THEOLOGY OF THE ICON
Volume I

THEOLOGY OF THE ICON
Volume 1

by

LEONID OUSPENSKY

translated by
ANTHONY GYTHIEL

with selections translated by
ELIZABETH MEYENDORFF

ST. VLADIMIR'S SEMINARY PRESS
CRESTWOOD, NY 10707–1699
1992

The publication of this book has been underwritten by a generous contribution by Dr. and Mrs. Demetre Nicoloff, Minneapolis, Minnesota.

Library of Congress Cataloging-in-Publication Data

Ouspensky, Léonide
    [Essai sur la théologie de l'icone dans l'Eglise orthodoxe. English]
    Theology of the icon / by Leonid Ouspensky; translated by Anthony Gythiel with selections translated by Elizabeth Meyendorff.
        p.   m.
    Vol. 1 is a rev. translation of: Essai sur la théologie de l'icône dans l'Eglise orthodoxe; v. 2 is a translation of: La théologie de l'icône; both were translated originally from Russian.
    Includes bibliographical references and index.
    ISBN 0-88141-122-1 (v. 1). — ISBN 0-88141-123-X (v. 2) — ISBN 0-88141-124-8 (set)
    1. Icons—cult. 2. Orthodox Eastern Church—Doctrines. 3. Orthodox Eastern Church and art. 4. Icon painting. I. Ouspensky, Léonide. Théologie de l'icône. English. 1992. II. Title.
BX378.5.O9713   1992   92-12323
246'.53—dc20   CIP

THEOLOGY OF THE ICON
Volume I

COPYRIGHT © 1978

by

ST VLADIMIR'S SEMINARY PRESS

Vol. 1 ISBN 0–88141–122–1
Set (Vol. I & II) ISBN 0–88141–124–8

PRINTED IN THE UNITED STATES OF AMERICA

Contents

Introduction

A large number of works about Christian sacred art exist in various languages. This art has been studied from the historical, aesthetic, sociological and archaeological points of view. All of these aspects are indeed components of sacred art. But they represent only its external side and are not concerned with its very essence, that is, that which this art conveys. At the same time, many works are dedicated to explaining the external and explicit connection of the image to the Holy Scriptures and to the other liturgical texts. Other works, finally, explain this art from a theological and philosophical point of view. But what does the Church itself think of the art which it has created? What are its teachings on this subject? How was sacred art understood by the holy councils and the Fathers who were concerned with it? All of this has not been the object of special attention. Moreover, as we shall see, certain authors go so far as to deny the Church's participation in the creation of its art. But can one imagine that the Church would neglect figurative art, at least as a strong means of influencing man? Figurative art was abundantly used in the paganism which surrounded the Church from the first centuries, and, later, by the Christian state. It is certain that the Church could not have ignored it. Its entire outlook on the image is a witness to this fact, and it is precisely with this that we shall begin our study.

It is well known that the veneration of holy icons plays a very important role in the Orthodox Church. The veneration of the icons of Christ, of the Virgin, of angels and of the saints is a dogma of the Christian faith formulated at the Seventh Ecumenical Council and proceeds from a basic doctrine of the Church: its confession of the Son of God who became man. His icon is a witness to the true and non-deceptive Incarnation of God. In the course of its history, the Church triumphed over heresy many times. But of all its victories, only the victory over iconoclasm, the victory of the icon, was solemnly proclaimed as the "Triumph of Orthodoxy," a victory which we celebrate each year on the first Sunday of Lent. This demonstrates the importance which the Church attributes to the image, and not just to any image, but to the specific image which it wrought in its fierce struggle against paganism, against iconoclasm and against other heresies, to the image which was paid for with the blood of a large number of martyrs and confessors.

Why does the Church attribute such a great importance to the icon? The icon is not just a simple image, nor a decoration, nor even an illustration of Holy Scripture. It is something greater. It is an object of worship and an integral part of the liturgy. The Church sees in its holy image not simply one of the aspects of Orthodox teaching, but the expression of Orthodoxy in its totality, the expression of Orthodoxy as such. The icon is one of the manifestations of the holy Tradition of the Church, similar to the written and oral traditions. As we shall see in our study, the "icon," according to the teaching of the Church, corresponds entirely to the "word" of Scripture. "That which the word communicates by sound, the painting shows silently by representation," says St Basil the Great.[1] And the Fathers of the Seventh Ecumenical Council repeat these words and specify that "through these two mediums which accompany each other. . . we acquire the knowledge of the same realities."[2]

It is absolutely impossible to imagine the smallest liturgical rite in the Orthodox Church without icons. The liturgical and sacramental life of the Church is inseparable from the image. Even before entering the sanctuary to celebrate the Divine Liturgy, the priest recites a prayer of purification before the Royal Doors (the central portal of the iconostasis) and a declaration of faith before the "local" icons. The icon is an object of worship embodying divine grace and forming an integral part of the liturgy. Often, and with good reason, the icon is called "theology in images." It is understandable that the basis of sacred art, its meaning and its content can only be a subject of theology similar to the study of the Holy Scripture. Therefore, one can neither understand nor explain sacred art outside of the Church and its life. Such an explanation would always be partial and incomplete. In relation to sacred art itself, it would be false.

1   *Hom. 19, On the 40 Martyrs,* PG 31: 509 A.
2   Mansi 13: 300 C.

In fact, sacred art not only reflects the life of the Church in all its complexity and in all its depth; it is an integral part of this life, just as a branch is a part of a tree. An object of worship, the icon is not merely provoked or inspired by the Liturgy: Together they form a homogeneous whole. The icon completes the Liturgy and explains it, adding its influence on the souls of the faithful. The contents and the meaning of the icon and of the Liturgy are the same, and this is why their form, their language, is also the same. It is the same symbolism, the same sobriety, the same depth in content. This is why, as everything in the Church, sacred art has a double dimension: Its very essence is unchangeable and eternal since it expresses the revealed truth, but at the same time it is infinitely diverse in its forms and expressions, corresponding to different times and places. Our study will therefore be, on the one hand and foremost, a theological study. On the other hand, on the historical and archaeological level, we will use the facts provided by secular archaeologists or historians of art.

The content and the meaning of sacred art determines one's attitude towards it. To understand this point more clearly, let us compare the attitudes of the Orthodox Church and of the Roman Catholic Church towards sacred art. The Roman Catholic Church confesses, as does Orthodoxy, the dogma of the veneration of icons. But its attitude towards sacred art differs considerably from the Orthodox attitude. Let us take as an example the decision of the Council of Trent, which has until now been the basis of all the regulations issued by the Vatican in the field of art. All these regulations have a negative tone: They pronounce what sacred art should not be. The following is the decision of the Council of Trent (1563, the twenty-fifth and last session):

> The Holy Council upholds that no image should be placed in the churches which is inspired by a false dogma and which can mislead the simple people; it wills that all impurity be avoided and that the images should not have any provocative attributes. To assure the regard to these decisions, the Holy Council prohibits any improper image from being placed anywhere, even in the churches which are not subject to the visit of the ordinary, unless the bishop has first approved it.[3]

This rule is repeated, some parts of it literally, in the new regulations

---

3   Quoted from E. Mâle, *L'art religieux après le Concile de Trente* (Paris, 1932), 1.

on the subject (June 30, 1952). These are the orders of a 1947 encyclical letter of Pius XII: "The field must be left absolutely open for the art of our time when it shows the respect and honor due to the buildings and the sacred rites. In such a way, it will enter into the wonderful concert which famous men have sung to the catholic faith in past centuries..."[4] The Pope adds that "everything which is not in accord with the holiness of the place" must be removed from the sanctuaries. As we see, neither the decision of the council, nor the papal encyclical letter of 1947, nor the other directives of the Roman Church set any criterion or indicate any connection with Tradition. They only indicate what should not be in sacred art, and this in not very clear terms. What is an "improper image"? What traits can be considered "provocative"? All of this remains unclear. Even in the West, this vagueness stirs up sharp criticisms which underline the negative aspect of rules pertaining to sacred art. Some have said concerning the regulations of 1952 that they preserve only a minimum of "tradition": just enough to keep the faithful from confusing a church steeple with a factory chimney. Otherwise they sanction all the mistakes of the past and of the present and proclaim that sacred art must search for a "new style." To participate in "the wonderful concert of famous men," as it is put by Pius XII, the Roman Church therefore appeals to the most famous of contemporary painters to decorate its churches, without being in the least concerned with whether they belong to the Church or not, or even if they are believers or atheists. How can there even be a question of intercourse between the image and the word of Scripture when the person who decorates a church or paints a sacred image is an atheist or when he belongs to another religion? One could in such a case speak only of a formal illustration of the letter of the scriptural text or, what would be even worse, of a personal interpretation by the painter, the application of his own ingenuity to a scriptural subject. This is being done in the field of art. This shows the extent to which the very meaning of the sacred image has been lost in the Roman Catholic Church.

This vagueness in the directives communicates the chaotic state of sacred art itself, which has now reached a critical point. In fact, the Roman Catholic Church has been forced to accept secular art, which often has a very doubtful spiritual content, or else to do without art

4   F. R. Regamey, *L'art sacré du XXe siècle* (Paris, 1952), 432.

altogether. For example, the following was written in an article which appeared several years ago in a French magazine:

> The Church [the Roman Catholic Church] finds itself today in the same situation as any individual. It must accept the criteria of pure aesthetics... Therefore the Church, unless it succumbs to sentimental bad taste, should either come to terms with the solutions reached by artists outside itself or else refrain from resorting to art.

The Orthodox Church, on the other hand, offers a positive teaching. It stipulates that artists paint icons as they were painted by the ancient and holy iconographers (see, for example, the Hundred Chapters Council in 1551). At first glance, this directive may appear to be very imprecise. But its entire significance becomes clear if one remembers the masterly expression of St Paul, quite relevant in its sobriety and power: "Be imitators of me," he wrote, "as I am of Christ" (1 Cor 11:1). To paint icons as they were painted by the ancient and holy iconographers means to follow Tradition and denotes a particular attitude towards sacred art. "Use colors according to Tradition," says St Symeon of Thessalonica. "This is true painting, as Scripture is its books..."[5] It is not a matter of copying the ancient iconographers. St Paul did not imitate Christ by copying His gestures and His words, but by integrating himself into His life, by letting Him live in him. Similarly, to paint icons as they were painted by the ancient iconographers does not mean to copy the ancient forms, since each historical period has its own forms. It means to follow the sacred Tradition, to live in the Tradition. But the power of Tradition is the power of the Holy Spirit and of continuity in the spiritual experience of the Church, the power of communion with the spiritual life of all the preceding generations back to the time of the apostles. In Tradition, our experience and our understanding are the experience and understanding of the Apostle Paul, of the holy iconographers and of the entire Church: We no longer live separately, individually, but in the Body of Christ, in the same total body as all of our brothers in Christ. This is in fact the case in all areas of spiritual life, but it is particularly true in that of sacred art. The contemporary iconographer must rediscover the internal outlook of the iconographers of old and be guided by the same living inspiration. He will then find true faithfullness to Tradition, which is not repetition but a

5 *Dialogue against heresies*, ch. 23, PG 155: 113 D.

new, contemporary revelation of the internal life of the Church. Indeed, an Orthodox iconographer faithful to Tradition always speaks the language of his time, expressing himself in his own manner, following his own way. We see, therefore, how the decisions of the Roman Church are vague in spite of their prolixity, and how the basic guidelines of the Orthodox Church are precise and concrete in their laconism.

We spoke briefly of the icon in the life of the Church, and we explained in a few words the importance which the Church ascribes to its sacred art. But if we now turn to the practice of the Church, we will frequently see a great discrepancy between the traditional teaching about the image and the image itself. We often see in our churches a large number of heteroclite, secular or semi-secular images which have little in common with the icon. These are, in fact, usually images of a secular art having merely a religious subject. Anything can be found, even Masonic symbols such as an eye in a triangle, called the "all-seeing eye." In most of our churches, true icons are lost amidst a multitude of representations foreign to Orthodoxy—these, so as not to be called simply Roman Catholic, are euphemistically characterized as "paintings in the Italian style" or icons "of the Italian genre." On the other hand, icons which are truly Orthodox are called "images of the Byzantine style," "Novgorodian," etc. One can speak of style in scientific analyses, in historical or archaeological studies, but to use this idea in the Church to characterize its art is as absurd as discussing the "style" in which the Creed or the Great Canon of St Andrew of Crete is written. It is clearly a meaningless statement. In the Church there is only one criterion: Orthodoxy. Is an image Orthodox or not? Does it correspond to the teaching of the Church or not? Style as such is never an issue in worship.

Many faithful believe that one can pray before any image, Orthodox or Roman Catholic, as long as there is an image, since it is only of secondary importance. This is why they bring all kinds of images into churches. Those who think in this way do not know that during the iconoclastic period of the eighth and ninth centuries, it was precisely this struggle for an authentic Orthodox image which called forth from the Church a large number of martyrs and confessors. Of course, one can pray before any image. One can also pray without any images at all, or even without a church. One can and one must pray always and everywhere. But this certainly does not mean that one can dispense with the Church and the image, or that the external appearance of the church and the images in it are a matter of indifference. One must not forget that when one enters a church, it is not only to pray in it. We also receive the teaching of Orthodoxy, and this beneficial teaching is our guide throughout our whole life, in addition to our prayers. It often happens in our churches that the sacred word is our guide and teaches us in a certain way, while the image, being heterodox, teaches us and guides us in a completely different way. How is this possible? We have preserved the Orthodox veneration of the image. But under the influence of Catholicism and Protestantism, we have become indifferent to the very contents of the image. This is why we can no longer distinguish the Roman Catholic image, which expresses, as we shall see, the Roman teaching, from the authentic Orthodox image. We accept everything and take a passive attitude toward the realm of sacred art.

Let us give several examples. There exists an opinion according to which nothing which has been used by the Church can be discarded. Human error is normal, but a theory based on an error and the erroneous practice which it produces are inadmissible in the Church. If this were not the case, we would not, for example, have any reason to reject the synodal regime in the Russian Church. Indeed, the regime lasted for many centuries, and the period was illumined by great saints, such as St Seraphim of Sarov, St Mitrofan of Voronezh, St Tikhon of Zadonsk and others. This same reference to practice is invoked in preserving iconographic subjects borrowed from heterodox art, based solely on the imagination of the artist, and which not only did not correspond to the Gospel but, on the contrary, contradicted it. These subjects are not rejected, since it is believed that the mere fact of their existence in our Church for two or three centuries is proof that they have become Orthodox. But time is not a criterion of truth. If a falsehood has been accepted for two hundred years, this does not mean that it has become a truth. And if it happens that the ecclesiastical authorities have been mistaken, then the Church always, in the end, corrects their error. Thus, a local council of Moscow in 1553-1554 accepted a representation borrowed from the West—the image of God the Father—under the pretext that this image had already been introduced into the practice of the Church. But in 1667, the Great

Council of Moscow considered the question from a different angle, asking whether or not this image corresponded to the Orthodox teaching. It reached the conclusion that it did not. The decision of the previous council was annulled, and this representation was forbidden.

On the other hand, even among the Orthodox there exist people who are disturbed by the Orthodox icon, believing as do some archaeologists and art historians that liturgical art is "medieval," "outdated," "idealistic," etc., and who are afraid of being left behind the times. But the opinion of scholars and philosophers of aesthetics cannot, as such, be an authority for the faithful. Often ignorant of the very basis of sacred art and applying secular standards to it, their views can only be unilateral and partial. It is amazing that those persons who are disturbed by the presence of icons are not, however, disturbed by the fact that our Liturgy goes back to the same times as does the icon and, to a great extent, even as far back as the Old Testament. But in spite of its antiquity, the Liturgy retains its fundamental importance, and very few consider it to be "outdated."

But the plague of our times is aestheticism. There is a dictatorship of "taste." Personal taste is usually accepted as the only criterion for the appreciation of a sacred image. One speaks of "good taste" and "bad taste." But in the Church, taste can be neither good nor bad and should not be used as a criterion. By what right should one person's taste be considered good and another's bad? By its very definition, taste is something subjective and changeable. For a sacred image, just as for the sacred writings, a relative and variable criterion cannot be valid. The notion of taste may apply to the artistic value of the image, but not to its value as a liturgical image. If one bases one's understanding exclusively on individual, aesthetic, or some other kind of appreciation, one reaches the point which St John of Damascus feared when he wrote: "If each person could act according to his desire, little by little, the entire body of the Church would be destroyed."[6] It is precisely in defending icons during the iconoclastic period in the eighth century that St John of Damascus wrote these words.

The Orthodox Church has always fought to defend its sacred art against secularization. Through the voice of its councils, its hierarchy and

6   *Third Treatise in the Defense of Holy Icons*, ch. 41, PG 94: 1356.

its faithful, it fought to retain the purity of the sacred image against the penetration of foreign elements characteristic of secular art. The Church did not fight for the artistic quality of its art, but for its authenticity, not for its beauty, but for its truth. It has retained unchanged the sacred tradition in art, the understanding of its dogmatic contents and of the spiritual significance of sacred art. We are constantly reminded of this in the Liturgy. It is, in particular, the stichera and canons of the feasts of the various icons (for example, that of the Holy Face on August 16, and especially the Liturgy of the Triumph of Orthodoxy) which uncover the meaning of the image in all its depth. But in times of spiritual decadence like our own, the voice of the Church is a voice which is not heard. Shamelessly, we listen without hearing the words which the Church proclaims, and we look without seeing, just as those of whom Christ speaks in His Gospel (Mt 13:13).

One must admit that the confusion existing in the Orthodox Church concerning sacred art is, to a large extent, a consequence of the education received by the clergy, which does not stress the priest's responsibility for the purity of the icon. Indeed, before his ordination, every priest promises to "obey all the rules established by the councils." But the learning which he acquires in religious institutions does not prepare him to be able to keep such a promise in the realm of sacred art. He is taught nothing about the theology of the image, though at the same time a future priest is taught archeology and art history. But these subjects cannot be useful unless they are limited to an auxiliary role. By themselves, without a theological basis, they give the future priest a false idea of what an image is in the Church. This is why, when a student becomes a priest, he is often incapable of distinguishing an icon from a secular image, or even certain icons from others, and of interpreting the representations of the principal feasts. How can he, under these circumstances, distinguish in an image the real from the false and explain to others the contents of the image? One usually replies that art is a special field, that to understand it one must be a specialized expert. Yes, certainly this is true when one is concerned with the historical or artistic aspect of the image. But if one is concerned with the contents, such a point of view is absolutely false. The icon, in fact, is art, but it is above all liturgical art, a part of the Liturgy. Thus, just as the celebrant should not be required to be a historian or a lover of literature in order to understand sacred Scripture, so also the understanding of the sacred image requires neither precise knowledge of art history nor the refinement of an aesthete. A priest should simply know how to "read" an icon as well as the Liturgy.

But whether priest or lay, we are all members of the Church. We are all called to witness to its truth in a world which does not understand it. This is why it is essential that each one of us be conscious of this truth in whatever form it is expressed, verbally or in images. The Orthodox teaching of the image was formulated several times, in response to errors and misunderstandings. These errors and misunderstandings repeat themselves, and our century has discovered nothing new in this field. The Orthodox Church has retained intact an immense richness not only in the realm of Liturgy and patristic thought, but also in that of sacred art, and we who enjoy the riches of this treasure should know about it and be witnesses to it. Those who confess Orthodoxy should be careful not to bring into the world a truth mixed with falsehood. Let us not forget that, just as thought in the realm of religion has not always reached the level of theology, so artistic creation has not always reached the level of authentic iconography. This is why one cannot consider every image, even one that is very old and very beautiful, as an infallible authority, especially if it originated in a time of decadence such as our own. Such an image may correspond to the teaching of the Church or it may not. It can deceive rather than teach. In other words, the teaching of the Church can be falsified by the image as much as by word. In the conditions existing today, we are facing a painful situation which leads to conflicts and polemics and often throws the faithful and particularly the painters into total confusion. Each one of us should be able, at every instant, to confess our faith by word and through the image.

The aim of this work, then, is to make known from a historical perspective the evolution of the icon and its content. Volume One is a revision of an earlier publication entitled *Essai sur la théologie de l'icône dans l'église orthodoxe* (Paris, 1960; trans., *Theology of the Icon* [New York: St Vladimir's Seminary Press, 1978]); Volume Two consists of various chapters published, in Russian, in *Messager de l'Exarchat du Patriarche russe en Europe occidentale.*

1

The Symbolism of the Church

Before we begin our discussion of the icon, it is necessary to consider briefly the whole of which it is a part: the church building and its symbolic significance.

What is symbolism? Symbolism expresses indirectly, through images, that which cannot be expressed directly in material or verbal forms. Being a mysterious language, symbolism also hides truths which it reflects from those who are not initiated and makes them understandable to those who know how to approach them. Everyday language frequently confuses the ideas of "sign" and "symbol," as if they were identical. In fact, there is a necessary spiritual distinction between them. A sign only portrays reality; a symbol always qualifies it in a certain way, bringing forth a superior reality. To understand a symbol is to participate in the presence; to understand a sign is to translate an indication. Let us take the example of the cross. In arithmetic, it is a sign of addition; as a road sign, it is a symbol which expresses and communicates the inexhaustible contents of Christianity.

In the Church, symbolism plays a very important role because the entire Church is, in a way, both material and spiritual. That which is material is directly accessible to us; that which is spiritual is indicated through symbols. The symbolism of the Church cannot be effectively studied outside of the Liturgy, because it is a liturgical symbolism and it is through the Liturgy that the Fathers explained it. Separated from the divine services, symbolism loses its meaning and becomes a series of sterile abstractions.

The word "Church" (in Greek ἐκκλησία) means "convocation" or "reunion." The Church "is thus named because it convokes all men and unites them with one another," says St Cyril of Jerusalem.[1] Other Fathers

1   *Catechetical Orations*, 18, 24 PG 33: 1044.

(for example, St Athanasius the Great, St John Chrysostom, St Augustine) express this same thought. The verb καλέω means "to summon;" ἐκκαλέω means "to convoke" from somewhere. Those who are called together are the apostles and the disciples of Christ, the new Israel. In the Old Testament, the people of Israel were distinct from the world so that they could announce to it the divine Incarnation and prepare the world for the coming of the Messiah. The new Israel—the Church—in turn brings the presence and the promise of the Kingdom of God to the fallen world; it prepares this world for Christ's Second Coming.

The word "Church" also designates the Body of Christ, His Kingdom made up of the communion of the faithful, and also the place of worship. In our prayers for the consecration of churches, the place of worship is, indeed, called the "house comparable to the heavens," "the image of the house of God." It is consecrated "to the image of the most holy Church of God, that is, of our very body which Thou deigneth to call Thy temple and the members of Thy Christ by the mouth of Thy glorious Apostle Paul," that is, to the image of the Church, the Body of Christ, according to the words of St Paul (Eph 1:23 and Col 1:18). Thus a church is an image, an icon, of the Church, the Body of Christ. It expresses symbolically that which cannot be expressed directly, because neither words nor direct images can represent the one, holy, catholic, and apostolic Church, the object of our faith but invisible in its fullness.

The foundation of Christian life has always been the same, both in the first centuries of our era and today. It is the birth of a new life, an intimate union with God which is essentially fulfilled in the sacrament of the Eucharist. A church, as the place where this sacrament is fulfilled and where men, united and revived, are gathered together, is different from all other places and buildings. It is characteristic that, among the various names which the first Christians gave to their temple, such as "church" or "the house of the Church," the most frequent designation was "the house of the Lord."[2] This name itself already underlies the difference between a church and all other buildings and expresses its specifically Christian meaning.

This meaning is connected with the heritage of the Old Testament.

2   H. Leclercq, *Manuel d'archéologie chrétienne*, vol. 1 (Paris, 1907), 361-2.

The tabernacle of the Old Testament, a prefiguration of the New Testament churches, was built according to the image shown to Moses on Mount Sinai. God Himself indicates both its general plan and its disposition in the smallest detail. The history of the Church shows us that the first Christians had not broken with the past. On the contrary, they believed themselves to be the direct heirs of the Old Testament. The Christians were the new Israel, the fulfillment of the prophecies. The Apostles and the Fathers constantly emphasized the traditional character of the new faith. The Apostles and the first Christians generally went to the synagogues and to the temple in Jerusalem and participated in Jewish worship. It is only after they were forbidden access to these places that they built Christian sanctuaries, and they did so in strict accord with the revealed character of the place of worship, with the very principle according to which the tabernacle and the Jerusalem temple had been built. But they also gave this principle its true meaning, as expressed in the New Testament and as the fulfillment of the prophecies. This is why one cannot doubt that the essential significance of a church, so directly connected with the very essence of Christianity, was understandable to everyone in the first centuries of our era, even though it was not immediately manifested in external or conceptual forms.

We learn from history and archaeology that the Christians of the first centuries did not only have catacombs and places of prayer in private homes, as we know from the Acts of the Apostles and the Epistles,[3] but that they also built churches above ground.[4] These churches were destroyed in the times of the persecutions; they were rebuilt. But in spite of the existence of these churches, neither the Fathers of the first centuries, nor writers in general, describe the Liturgy extensively or dwell upon its meaning or the symbolism of the church. There are two reasons for this silence: (1) There was no need to write about that which everyone understood, that which everyone lived; (2) Christians did not want to initiate the pagans into their sacraments, to lay bare their faith and their hope. The truths of the faith were confessed by life itself and needed no formulation.

3 Acts 12:12, 20:7-8; Rom 16:4; 1 Cor 16:19; Col 4:15.
4 H. Leclercq, vol. 1, 378ff; Sisto Scaglia, *Manuel d'archéologie chrétienne* (Turin, 1916), 143-144.

There exist, nevertheless, some indications dating back to the first centuries, showing how early Christians understood their place of worship. According to the *Didascalia* and the *Apostolic Constitutions*, a church should remind the faithful of a boat. We know that the Fathers frequently used the image of the boat and, particularly, that of Noah's ark to symbolize the Church. Noah's ark was seen as a prefiguration of the Church: Just as this ark was a refuge during the flood, so the Church, guided by the Holy Spirit through the tides of life, is a salutary refuge for Christians. Even today, we continue to call the central part of our churches "the nave," from the Latin *navis*, ship. Symbolic images of Noah's ark can be found in ancient monuments, in the form of a square box,[5] sometimes with a dove flying above it. Archaeological diggings show that many churches in the first centuries were built in a square shape, that is, in the image of the ark. At first sight, this analogy may appear to be artificial, but for the small Christian communities, surrounded by a more or less hostile paganism, the Church was indeed an ark, where salvation could be found in the sacraments.

From the fourth century on, Christian authors begin to explain the symbolism of the church in more detail. Two particular circumstances made such explanations necessary:

(1) In the fourth century, under St Constantine, the Church received the right to legitimate existence in the Roman Empire. This historical event, of capital, importance led to the triumph of the Church and had very important consequences for its art. Construction and adornment of the churches was developed to a point unknown until that time. The famous church historian Eusebius of Caesarea speaks at length and very enthusiastically about these structures. A large multitude of recent converts filled these new churches. Most of them needed spiritual guidance and direct explanation of the Christian faith. One of the ways this instruction was accomplished was through the symbolism of the churches and of worship, which was now explained in detail.

(2) In the fourth century, Christian worship took more precise and determined forms. The liturgies of both St John Chrysostom and St Basil the Great date to this time. The rapid progress in the definition of rites

---

5   H. Leclercq, vol. 1, 395.

and in the decoration of churches can be seen in a description by Eusebius
of the reign of St Constantine:

> A clear and luminous day, without even the smallest cloud, illuminates with rays
> of divine light the churches of Christ in the whole universe... Churches are again
> rebuilt to a great height and have a much better appearance than the ancient,
> destroyed churches... Feasts of renovation and consecration of new churches are
> beginning to be celebrated in the town... The worship which is celebrated by the
> priest and the sacred rites become more perfect, the customs of worship become
> more beautiful.[6]

Certain ancient liturgies (for example, the Syriac text of the Liturgy of St
James) contained commentaries for the instruction and guidance of the
faithful. These commentaries were part of the liturgical text and were read
by the deacon during the celebration. It is believed that these commentaries were introduced at the end of the third or in the beginning of the
fourth centuries, that is, at the time when they were made necessary by the
large number of new converts in the Church. This makes us think that
today, too, such commentaries would not be superfluous, at least during
a sermon.

What is the basis of the symbolism in churches? Christian life is based
on two essential realities. One is the redeeming sacrifice of Christ, the
need to participate in this sacrifice, to partake of communion in it in
order to be saved. The other essential truth is the goal and the result of
this sacrifice: the sanctification of man, and with him, of the whole visible
world, resulting in peace between God and the world. This second truth
is the main subject of Church symbolism, which points to the forthcom-
ing universal Kingdom of God. It is precisely this orientation toward the
future, this building up of the future, which distinguished Christian
worship from all others.

Worship can be celebrated in different languages and can take many
forms. Similarly, a church can be shaped like a cross, a basilica or a
rotunda. It can be built according to the tastes and the ideas of any epoch
or of any civilization, but its meaning was, is, and will always be the same.
Each people leaves its characteristic traits in the construction of churches.
But this diversity of forms only serves to emphasize the unity of meaning,
the confession of the same truth.

6   *Ecclesiastical History* X, 1 and 2, PG 20:845A, 845C and 848B.

In a homily on the consecration of a church in Tyre at the beginning of the fourth century, Eusebius already devotes a rather detailed passage to the symbolism of the building. His fundamental thought is that, in a church, what we see is identical to what we hear. The building corresponds to the worship which we celebrate in it. It is the house of God, for God lives in it with the faithful, the receivers of His Spirit. It is the heavens on earth, it is already the earth of the time to come, when God will be all in all. The beauty of a church reveals, in a way, the beauty of the celestial Jerusalem which God prepares for those who love Him.[7] But Eusebius does not limit himself to commenting on the church as a whole. He already provides several explanations of its parts: the sanctuary, separated by a barrier, the nave and the narthex.

It is particularly in the seventh and eighth centuries that the symbolism of the churches acquires its most complete theoretical expression. The most systematic commentaries can be found in the *Mystagogy* of St Maximus the Confessor (seventh century), who also left us a remarkable study of the Liturgy; in the writings of St Sophronius, Patriarch of Jerusalem (seventh century); in those of St Germanus, Patriarch of Constantinople (d. 740), an important confessor of Orthodoxy during the iconoclastic period; and in the words of St Simeon, Archbishop of Thessalonica (fifteenth century). The seventh and eighth centuries, when symbolism became so popular, are also the time of vigorous liturgical creativity, the time of the great hymnographers, St Andrew of Crete, St Cosmas of Maium and St John of Damascus.

When one studies these commentaries, one must never forget that they do not express the subjective opinion of the authors. The symbolism of the Church is objectively based on the essence of Christianity. It expresses a well-defined reality, the liturgical life, i.e., one of the principal aspects of Tradition. This is why St Simeon of Thessalonica begins his *Book on the Church* with the words:

> With love, we pass on to you that which we have taken from the Fathers. For we offer nothing new, but only that which has been passed on to us, and we have changed nothing but we have retained everything, like a creed, in the state in which it has been given to us. We worship exactly as Christ Himself did and as did the apostles and the Fathers of the Church.[8]

7   *Ecclesiastical History* X, 4, PG 20: 873.
8   PG 155: 701AB.

This presents a striking parallel with theological thought, in which the Fathers also tried to avoid all individual and subjective valuation. "I pray God so as not to think or to pronounce on Him, as did Solomon, anything which comes from me personally," writes St Gregory Nazianzen.[9]

St Maximus the Confessor and St Sophronius see in the church the image of the spiritual and visible worlds, the image of that which we perceive spiritually and that which we perceive with our senses. They particularly emphasize the cosmic importance of a church, as an image of the entire created but transfigured world.

St Germanus speaks of the Church as the Body of Christ and of the church as a place of worship in the same terms and in the same sentence, thus emphasizing that the latter is but an image of the former. He says: "The Church is the heavens on earth, where God, who is higher than the heavens, lives." He continues: "It is reminiscent of the crucifixion, the burial and the resurrection of Christ; it is more glorified than the tabernacle of the Covenant," which obviously refers to the place of worship. "It was prefigured in the patriarchs, based on the apostles...it was announced by the prophets, adorned by the hierarchs, sanctified by the martyrs, and its altar is founded on their holy relics." Having clearly emphasized the analogy between the Church, the Body of Christ, and a church as the place of worship, St Germanus goes on to explain the meaning of the place of worship:

> The church is a divine house where the mysterious and vivifying sacrifice is fulfilled; it contains the interior sanctuary, the holy cave, the sepulcher, the meal which saves and vivifies the soul; it is the place where you will find the pearls of the divine dogmas which the Lord taught unto His disciples.

St Simeon of Thessalonica also emphasizes this significance of the church and specifies, among other things, that the most solemn rite of the consecration of a church presents it to us as "a mysterious heaven and the Church of the first-born." It is obvious that the Church about which the Fathers speak is not only the terrestrial Church in its present state, but it is also the celestial Church which is intricately connected with it; in other words, the Kingdom of God which will come in its power when God will be "all in all" (Eph 1:23). This is what the church expresses. St Simeon of

9 *Hom. 20, On the Trinity,* PG 35: 1069C.

Thessalonica calls a church "paradise," and the "gifts of paradise," for it contains not the tree of life, but life itself, which acts in the sacraments and is communicated to the faithful.

Thus, a church is a very complex reality, having a meaning rich in content. It is a sacred place where the members of the Church commune in the divine life through the sacraments. Being the first fruits of the Kingdom to come, it is both a part of this Kingdom, as it already exists on the earth, and an anticipation of its coming in glory. It is an image of the divine Kingdom, toward which the Church leads the world.

But patristic commentaries do not limit themselves to explaining the symbolism of the church building. They also clarify the meaning of each of its parts. The patristic conception of a church and of its parts is well summarized in a contemporary work, Archbishop Benjamin's *Novaia Skrizhal'* ("New Table of the Law"). The church can be divided into three parts (the sanctuary, the nave and the narthex), according to the plan of the tabernacle of Moses and the temple of Solomon. Just as the people of Israel, the Church of the Old Testament, prefigured the Church of the New Testament, so also the tabernacle and the temple prefigured the sacred places of the New Covenant, which have preserved the same plan (Fig. 1). St Simeon of Thessalonica is reminded of the Holy Trinity by this tripartition of the three orders of the celestial hierarchs and of the Christian people themselves, who are divided into three categories: the clergy, the faithful, and the penitents and catechumens.

The sanctuary is reserved for the clergy. It is the most important part of the church, where the sacrament of the Eucharist is performed, and corresponds to the holy of holies in the tabernacle. Symbolically, the sanctuary represents the house of God, "the heaven of the heavens," according to St Simeon of Thessalonica. According to the words of St Germanus, it is "the place where Christ, King of all things, rules with the apostles." The sanctuary is usually in the eastern part of the building, so that the whole church faces east. This orientation also has a symbolic significance. On the one hand, the lost paradise was "in the East." On the other hand, and more important, the coming of the Kingdom is often identified with the sunrise: Christ is glorified as "the Orient from on high." This Kingdom of God to come is often seen, particularly in the first centuries of Christianity, as "the eighth day" of creation. The coming

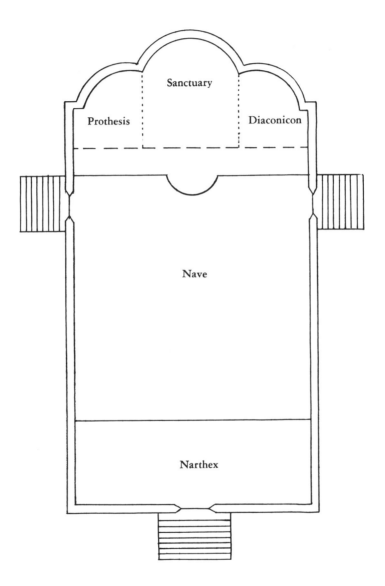

1. Plan of an Orthodox Church

of this "day without end," which we await and prepare for, its rising, as it were, is symbolized by the sunrise in the east. This is why St Basil stipulates, in his canon 90, that our prayers should always be oriented towards the east, where the sun rises.

The central part of the church, the nave, corresponds to the "holy" of the tabernacle, which was separated from the courtyard by a veil. Every day, the Jewish priests would enter it to bring the sacrifices. In the Church of the New Testament, it is the faithful laypeople, "the royal priesthood, the holy people," according to the expression of St Paul, who enter into this part and pray to God. This part of the church is therefore for those persons who are enlightened by the faith and who are preparing themselves to partake in the grace of the eucharistic sacrament. Having received this grace, they are redeemed and sanctified; they are the Kingdom of God. If the sanctuary represents that which goes beyond the created world, the house of God Himself, then the nave of the church represents the created world. But it is a world which is justified, sanctified and deified; it is the Kingdom of God, the new earth and the new heavens. This is how the Fathers describe this part of the church. St Maximus the Confessor, for example, says the following:

> Just as, in man, the carnal and spiritual principles are united, even though the carnal principle does not absorb the spiritual, nor does the spiritual principle absorb the carnal into itself, but rather spiritualizes it, so that the body itself becomes an expression of the spirit, so also in a church, the sanctuary and the nave communicate: the sanctuary enlightens and guides the nave, which becomes its visible expression. Such a relationship restores the normal order of the universe, which had been destroyed by the fall of man. Thus it reestablishes what had been in paradise and what will be in the Kingdom of God.[10]

The narthex, finally, corresponds to the courtyard of the tabernacle, the external part, which was reserved for the people. Today, the sanctified people stand in the nave, and it is the catechumens and penitents who remain in the narthex, that is, those who are only preparing themselves to enter the Church and those whom the Church places in a special category and who are not permitted to partake in the communion of the holy gifts. This is why, once the sacrament is fulfilled, those who do not partake of it are asked to leave, some because they are not yet members of the

10 *Mystagogy*, chs. 8-21, PG 91: 672.

Church and others because they have fallen away or are considered unworthy. Thus the very plan of a church makes a clear distinction between those who participate in the Body of Christ and those who do not. The latter are not driven out of the church and can remain until a certain moment. But they cannot participate in the internal, sacramental life of the Church. They are neither completely outside the church, nor a part of it. They are, so to speak, on the periphery, at the limit between the Church and the world. The narthex, according to the Fathers, symbolizes the unredeemed part of the world, the world lying in sin, and even hell. It is always at the end of the church opposite from the sanctuary, that is, at the west end.

A "temporal" significance, which changes during the different moments of worship, is added to the "spatial" and permanent significance of a church. The Church also uses images in order to show that a church, a place of worship, is an image of the one, holy, catholic and apostolic Church, that it is the real first fruits and the image of the Kingdom of God to come, and in order to make this image more precise, by suggesting the presence of this Kingdom to come. The iconographic subjects are distributed according to the meaning of each part of a church and its role in worship. If the symbolism of the Liturgy was explained by the Fathers during the pre-iconoclastic period, in contrast, it is after the iconoclastic period that the relationship between the decoration of the church and this symbolism was made more specific. The decoration acquired the forms of a clear and precise theological system.

We will speak here only in very general terms of the classical plan of decoration which prevailed from the ninth century, that is, from the post-iconoclastic period, when the system of decorating of churches was definitely established, until the end of the seventeenth century. Obviously, this stability and uniformity exists only in the general shape of the decoration, not in its details.

In the sanctuary, the first row of paintings, beginning from the bottom, represents the Fathers, authors of liturgies, and with them the other holy hierarchs and deacons in their rank of concelebrants. Above these, the Eucharist itself is represented in the form of bread and wine. Above the Eucharist, the image of the Mother of God is placed directly behind the altar. Her place, close to the sacrament, corresponds to her place in the eucharistic canon where, immediately after the epiclesis, she is mentioned at the head of the entire Church. At the same time, the Mother of God personifies the Church itself, because she contained in herself the Creator of the world whom the whole world cannot contain. This is why, in this part of the sanctuary, she is usually represented in the *orante* position, that is, interceding before God for the sins of the world, which is simultaneously her role and the role of the Church. This representation of the Virgin praying in the very place where the sacrifice is fulfilled reflects a very special meaning. The uplifted hands are a gesture which completes the sacrifice. This is why the priest also makes this same gesture during the Liturgy. This position of uplifted hands is not a formal requirement, but it has become deeply rooted in the Liturgy, as it is bound to the sacrifice and is the image of prayer itself.

Because the sanctuary is the place where the unbloody sacrifice established by Christ is offered, the image of Christ is placed above that of the Virgin. It is He who is Himself the offered sacrifice and the Sanctifier who offers, and His image has a uniquely eucharistic significance here. Finally, Pentecost is represented in the vault. This image indicates the presence of the Holy Spirit, through whom the sacrament of the Eucharist is fulfilled.

This very brief survey permits us to see the capital importance of the sanctuary: It is the place which sanctifies the entire church. When the Royal Doors are opened during the Liturgy, it is as if the heavens themselves were opened a bit, permitting us to catch a glimpse of their splendor.

The nave of the church, as we already know, symbolizes the transfigured creation, the new earth and the new heavens, and at the same time, the Church. This is why the leader of the Church, Christ the Pantocrator, is painted in the dome. The Church had been announced by the prophets and was established on the apostles; they are represented immediately under the image of Christ. They are followed, in the four corners, by the four evangelists, who announced the good news and preached the Gospel in the four parts of the world. The columns which support the building are decorated with the images of the pillars of the Church: the martyrs, the hierarchs and the ascetics. The most important events of sacred history are found everywhere on the walls, particularly those events which the liturgical feasts celebrate, the "pearls of divine dogmas," in the words of St Germanus of Constantinople. Finally, on the western wall, the Last

Judgment is presented: the end of church history and the beginning of the age to come.

Thus, the decoration of Orthodox churches does not depend on the individual conception of artists. The iconographic themes are distributed according to the meaning of the church as a whole and the meaning of each of its parts.

The Church of the Old Testament, as well as all other religions, used symbols. This symbolism prefigured the coming of Christ. But Christ has come, and, nevertheless, the symbolism inherited from Israel continues to exist in the new Church, as an indispensable part of its worship, penetrating the entire Liturgy with its words, its gestures and its images. This symbolism is an initiation into the mysteries which are fulfilled in the Church and the revelation of a reality which is always present in it and which cannot be expressed directly. This reality is the Kingdom of God, whose authentic first-fruits are present as a spiritual, material and physical reality in the Eucharist, the central sacrament of the Church. For "it is impossible for us to raise ourselves to the contemplation of spiritual objects without some kind of intermediary, and to lift ourselves, we need something which is close and familiar to us," says St John of Damascus.[11] In other words, worship, and everything which is a part of it, is a path toward our sanctification, toward our deification. Everything in a church is oriented toward this goal. After the Fall, the Old Testament was the first step, but it was not yet a direct preparation for the age to come; it was only the preparation for the second stage, that of the New Testament. That which was, in the Old Testament, the future, has now become the present; and this present, in turn, prepares and leads us to that which is still to come, the celestial Jerusalem. Here is how St John of Damascus understands the Epistle to the Hebrews:

> Notice that the law and everything that was established by the law, as well as the whole worship which we now offer up, are sacred things made by man which, through the intermediary of matter, we lift towards the immaterial God. The law and everything that was established by the law [that is, the entire Old Testament] was a prefiguration of our present worship. And the worship which we presently offer up is an image of the things to come. These things [that is,

---

11 *First Treatise in the Defense of Holy Icons*, ch. 2 PG 94: 1233.

reality itself] are the celestial, immaterial Jerusalem which is not made by the hand of man, according to the words of the Apostle, "for here we have no lasting city, but we seek the city which is to come" [Heb 13:14], that is, the celestial Jerusalem of which God is the "builder and maker" [Heb 11:10]. Indeed, everything that was established both by the law and by our present worship only exists in relation to the celestial Jerusalem.[12]

A church is, therefore, the prefiguration of the peace to come, of the new heavens, and of the new earth where all creatures will gather around their Creator. The construction and decoration of churches is based on this image. The Fathers do not stipulate any style of architecture; they do not indicate how the building should be decorated and how icons should be painted. Everything flows from the general meaning of the church and follows a rule of art which is analogous to the rule of liturgical creativity. In other words, we have a very clear, albeit general, formula which guides the architect and the artist, while leaving him the freedom of the Holy Spirit. This formula is passed on from generation to generation by the living Tradition of the Church, the Tradition which dates back not only to the apostles but even to the Old Testament. If we live in this Tradition, we can understand the Church as it was understood by our holy Fathers, and we will decorate it accordingly. If we move away from this Tradition, we can introduce into our churches elements which do not correspond to the Church's very nature, but which reflect only our everyday life. Thus, we secularize the Church.

The very meaning of the church, its *raison d'être*, requires it to be different from all other buildings. According to the words of Jesus Christ Himself, His Church is a Kingdom "which is not of this world." However, the Church lives in the world and for the world, for its salvation. This is the goal of its existence. Being the "Kingdom which is not of this world," it has its own nature which is distinct from the world. And it can fulfill its goal only by remaining faithful to its specific nature, to itself. Its way of life, its actions and methods, are different from those of the world. Its art, in particular, does not resemble the art of the world. It expresses different kinds of truths and has other goals. If it mingles with secular art, it no longer corresponds to the goal which it must serve.

From the first centuries, the Christian Church established the interior

12   *Second Treatise in the Defense of Holy Icons*, ch. 23, PG 94: 1309.

aspect of its temples, the character of the sacred images, the hymns, the sacerdotal vestments, etc. All this forms a harmonious whole, a perfect unity and a liturgical fullness in the Church and in the Liturgy. This unity, this convergence toward the same goal, implies that each of the elements which make up the divine service is subordinate to the general meaning of the church and, consequently, no element has value in itself alone. Images and hymns express, each in their own way, the same transfigured universe and prefigure the same peace to come.

United by this common goal, these different elements which enter into worship realize this "unity in diversity" and this "richness in unity" which express, both as a whole and in every detail, the catholicity of the Orthodox Church, its *sobornost'*. They create the beauty of the church which is so different from the beauty of the world because it reflects the harmony of the age to come. As an example, one can remember the Russian chronicler's account of the conversion of St Prince Vladimir. When his messengers, whom he had sent to Constantinople as part of his program of comparing the different religions, returned, they told of how, when they were participating in a Liturgy at St Sophia, they no longer knew whether they were on earth or in heaven. Even if this is only a legend, it corresponds perfectly to the Orthodox understanding of beauty. The imperial palace was also beautiful, but it did not leave the same impression on the messengers of St Vladimir.

All of this of course is not new, but the obvious experience of one who lives in the Church. The Church never loses this Tradition, and reminds us of it constantly by the Liturgy, by the voice of its councils, by its hierarchs and its faithful. Thus, in 1945, the Patriarch of Moscow, Alexis, called us to Tradition by writing the following to the clergy of Moscow:

> So as to indicate what true beauty is in the church, in worship, and, in particular, in liturgical music, not according to my personal taste but in the very spirit of the Church, I wish to give the following directions, which are indispensable for all priests and for all churches.
>
> In a church, everything is different from that which we constantly see around us and in our homes. The images are not the same as those we have in our homes. The walls are painted with sacred images; everything shines brightly; everything raises the spirit and removes it from the usual thoughts and impressions of this world. And when we see in a church something which does not correspond to its greatness and its meaning, we are shocked. The holy Fathers, who not only

established the rite and the worship, but also the external aspect and the internal arrangement, thought of everything. They foresaw and ordered everything so as to create in the faithful a special spiritual state, so that nothing impedes their flight toward the heavens, toward God, toward the celestial world whose reflection a church should be. If in a hospital everything is directed toward treating the maladies of the body, and conditions are created which correspond to the needs of the sick person, so in a spiritual hospital, a church of God, one should also provide all the things that are needed.[13]

In his message, the late patriarch particularly emphasized music, which, just like the image, is one of the grave questions of our day. "To sing liturgical hymns in the shrill manner of worldly songs or of the passionate tunes of opera is to deprive the faithful of any possibility of concentrating, as well as of grasping the contents and the meaning of the hymns." However beautiful these songs and these tunes may be in themselves, they do not fulfill the purpose of church singing. The same can be said about images. Of course, each one of us has his habits and his tastes. But in church we must learn to transcend them and to sacrifice them. Moreover, the role of a church is not at all to satisfy the habits and tastes of some individual; it consists in directing him or her on the saving path of Christ.

The symbolism of the church shows us the foundation on which the symbolic language of worship, and, in particular, of the icon, is based—this language which we have unfortunately forgotten. All the testimonies of the Fathers and of the ecclesiastical writers which we have mentioned are only a few expressions of that by which the Church has lived from its beginning and by which it will live until the Second Coming of Christ.

The direct image is a characteristic trait of the New Testament. This New Testament image will not disappear until the coming of the reality which it prefigures: the Kingdom of God. But as long as we are still on the way, as long as the Church is still only building this Kingdom to come, we will continue to live in the realm of the image. It is through the image that the Church shows us the way toward our goal.

We could not participate in the building up of the Kingdom of God, we could not ask in all good conscience, "Thy Kingdom come," if we had

---

13 "Paschal Message to the Rectors of the Churches in Moscow," *Calendar of the Patriarchate of Moscow for 1947* (in Russian).

no idea of what this Kingdom will be. The symbolism of an Orthodox church and, in particular, of an icon is an authentic reflection, though of course a very weak one, of the glory of the age to come. In the words of St Symeon the New Theologian:

> God can be known to us in the same way as a man can see an endless ocean by standing at the shore at night with a dimly lit candle. Do you think he can see much? Not much, almost nothing. And nevertheless, he sees the water well. He knows that there is an ocean in front of him, that this ocean is huge and that he cannot see it all at once. The same is true of our knowledge of God.[14]

---

14 Oration 61, *Works* (Moscow, 1892—in Russian), 100.

2

Origins of the Christian Image

The word "icon" derives from the Greek word εἰκών, meaning "image" or "portrait." When the Christian image was being created in Byzantium, this term was used for all representations of Christ, the Virgin, a saint, an angel or an event from sacred history, whether this image was painted or sculpted,[1] mobile or monumental, and whatever the technique used. Now this term is used by preference to designate portable works of painting, sculpture, mosaic, and the like. This is the meaning given to the icon in archaeology and history of art. In the Church, we also make a distinction between a wall-painting and an icon. A wall-painting, whether it is a fresco or a mosaic, is not an object by itself, but is a part of the architecture, while an icon painted on a board is itself an object of art. But in principle, their meaning is the same. They are distinguished not by their significance but by their use and purpose. Thus, when we speak of icons, we will have in mind all sacred images, whether they are paintings on boards, frescoes, mosaics or sculptures. In any case, the English word "image," just as the Russian word *obraz*, embraces all these meanings.

We must first make a brief comment about the different points of view concerning the origin of Christian art and attitude of the Church toward it in the first centuries. Such points of view have indeed led to different evaluations. There are, on the one hand, the scientific points of view which are numerous, fluctuating and often contradictory. They are sometimes close to the attitude of the Church, and are sometimes opposed to it. On the other hand, there is the attitude of the Church, which is unique and has never changed from the beginning until now. The Orthodox Church maintains and teaches that the sacred image has existed from the beginning of Christianity. Far from being opposed to the latter, the image

---

1 One must note that, contrary to current opinion, the Orthodox Church never forbade the use of statues; such a negative prescription would have no basis in the teaching of the Church.

is, on the contrary, its indispensable attribute. The Church declares that the icon is an outcome of the Incarnation; that it is based upon this Incarnation and therefore belongs to the very essence of Christianity, and cannot be separated from it.

Points of view that contradict this statement of the Church became widespread from the eighteenth century on. The English scholar Gibbon (1737–1791), author of *The History of the Decline and Fall of the Roman Empire*, maintained that the first Christians had an insurmountable aversion to the use of images. According to him, this aversion was a consequence of their Jewish origin. Gibbon believed that the first icons appeared only in the beginning of the fourth century. This opinion was accepted by many, and Gibbon's ideas have unfortunately been upheld, in one form or another, until the present day.

It cannot be doubted that certain Christians, especially those coming from Judaism and relying on the Old Testament interdiction, denied the very possibility of the image in Christianity; and this all the more since the Christian communities were surrounded on all sides by a paganism whose influence was still felt. These Christians, taking into account their ill-fated experience of paganism, made an effort to keep their religion from being contaminated by idolatry, which could encroach upon it by way of artistic creation. Iconoclasm must have been as old as the cult of images. All this is easily understood, but it could not have played a decisive role in the Church, as we shall see.

According to modern scholarship, the aversion of the first Christians toward images is based upon the texts of certain ancient authors[2] directed against art, such authors being qualified as "Fathers of the Church." A clarification is needed: since an ecclesiastical term ("Fathers of the Church") is used, it is important not to deviate from its proper meaning. Now, in spite of the respect the Church has for some of these ancient authors who occupy the central place in the scholarly argumentation (Tertullian, Origen and Eusebius), it does not view them as being truly Orthodox.[3] Thus, one

---

2   Especially Tertullian (160–240/250), Clement of Alexandria (150–216), Origen (185/186–254/255), Eusebius of Caesarea (265–399/340) and others who are less well-known, such as Minutius Felix (second or third centuries), Arnobius (255/260–327), and Lactantius (240/250–?).

3   Despite all his greatness as an apologist and confessor, Tertullian ended his life in a Montanist sect; his *De Pudicitia*, in which he protests against certain images, was written after he had

attributes to the Church an attitude which it does not recognize as being its own. At the most, the writings of these authors can be acknowledged as expressions of their personal convictions, and as reflecting certain trends in the Church that were antagonistic toward images. But they cannot be recognized as Church Fathers, and this is not merely a semantic quarrel: by calling such writers "Fathers of the Church," one identifies their attitude with that of the Church, the spokesmen of which they would have been, and one concludes that it is the Church itself that was opposed to images for fear of idolatry.

"Christian art is born outside the Church and, at least at the beginning, developed almost against its will. Christianity, springing from Judaism, was naturally, like the religion from which it arose, hostile to idolatry." The author concludes:

> The Church did not create Christian art. In all probability, it did not retain an indifferent and uninterested attitude towards it for long; in accepting it, the Church most probably restricted it in certain ways, but it was created upon the initiative of the faithful.[4]

The penetration of images into worship is viewed as a phenomenon that escaped the control of the Church and is, in the best of cases, due to indecision, to the vacillation of the hierarchy when confronted by this "paganization" of Christianity. If art appeared in the Church, it is despite the latter. "One will certainly not be wrong in dating the general reversal of the Church on the question of images to between 350 and 400," Th. Klauser writes.[5] Thus, according to modern scholarship, there is, on the one hand, the Church, represented by the hierarchy and the clergy and, on the other, the faithful, and it is precisely the faithful who would have imposed the image upon the hierarchy. By identifying the Church only

    already left the Church. Origen was condemned by the Fifth Ecumenical Council; Eusebius, a semi-Arian, was also an Origenist.

4   L. Bréhier, *L'Art chrétien* (Paris, 1928), 13, 16. In the same order of ideas, see, for example, the famous *Dictionnaire d'Archéologie Chrétienne et de Liturgie* by F. Cabrol (Paris, 1915); Ch. Diehl, *Manuel d'Art byzantin* vol. 1 (1925), 1, 360; the official Encyclopedia of the Roman Church entitled *Ecclesia* (Paris, 1927), 611; L. Réau, *L'Art du Moyen âge*, coll. "L'évolution de l'humanité" (Paris, 1935), 2, 3; V. Lazarev, *History of Byzantine Painting* vol. 1 (in Russian) (Moscow-Leningrad, 1947), 41; A. Grabar, *L'iconoclasme byzantin* (Paris, 1957), the chapter entitled "L'Eglise et les images." Among the most recent authors, let us mention Th. Klauser, "Die Äusserungen der alten Kirche zur Kunst," *Gesammelte Arbeiten zur Liturgie-Geschichte* (Münster, 1974), 329–37.

5   *Ibid.*, 334.

with the hierarchy, one contradicts the concept of the Church as it was in the first Christian centuries, and as it always is in Orthodoxy. The body of the Church is formed by the clergy and the faithful *together*.

This theory also contradicts the material data we possess. Indeed, the existence of frescoes in the catacombs from the first century on is well known, namely in places of assembly and worship, and where the clergy were buried (for example, in the catacomb of Callistus). Such images were therefore known not only to the faithful but also to the hierarchy. It is hard to imagine that the clergy did not see them and that, if Christianity was incompatible with art, it did not take any measures to put an end to this error.[6]

The iconoclastic attitude of certain ancient authors and the prejudice against images within certain trends among Christians of our time (Protestantism, for example) have led to an identification of the Christian image with the idol. This confusion has, with great thoughtlessness, been attributed to the ancient Church for which, still according to these modern authors, the Old Testament interdiction remained valid. But no Orthodox believer could accept the confusion between icon and idol. We know, indeed, that the Church during its long history has invariably drawn a very clear line between the two. Proofs for this are found in the works of ancient authors or in the first-century saints' lives or later.

As to the ancient authors, even when one admits that their opposition to images was real (as was the case with Eusebius), such opposition only proves the existence and role of the image, for one does not fight against that which does not exist or is of no importance. But most of them, while protesting against images, clearly had in mind only pagan images. Thus, Clement of Alexandria, among those who are viewed as the most unrelenting adversaries of Christian images, writes:

> Art has another illusion with which to beguile; for it leads you on, though not to be in love with the statues and paintings, yet to honor and worship them. The painting, you say, is lifelike. Let the art be praised, but let it not beguile man by

6   It is true that modern scholarship tends not to follow the dating made by scholars in the past; on the contrary, it redates the frescoes in the catacombs in terms of its own scientific procedures. Thus, Th. Klauser believes that the dating should be modified so as to adapt it to the observations he develops. This is what is actually done. See, for example, the journal *Les Dossiers de l'Archéologie*, no 18 (1977), where the same frescoes are attributed either to the second or to the fourth century, depending on the scientific method of the authors.

pretending to be truth.[7]

Thus, Clement speaks only of images that "fascinate and deceive," presenting themselves as the truth; he is opposed merely to false, deceiving art. Elsewhere he writes:

> We are permitted to have a ring to make a seal. The images which are engraved on it and which we use as a seal should preferably be a dove, a fish, or a ship with unfurled and rapid sails; one can even represent a lyre as did Polycrates or an anchor as did Seleucus; finally, one could represent a fisherman at the seashore, the sight of which would remind us of the apostle and the children drawn out from the waters [i e , the newly baptized].[8]

All of these images are Christian symbols. It is obvious that two very different kinds of images are being spoken of—images that are desirable and useful to Christians, and others which are false and inadmissible. Besides, Clement himself specifies this by criticizing Christians who, on their seals, engrave images of pagan gods, on their swords and arrows images of the goddess of war, on their goblets images of Bacchus, etc.—all representations which are incompatible with Christianity. All of this bears witness to a prudent and vigilant attitude towards the image on the part of Clement. It is true that he only speaks of its secular use, and says nothing about the liturgical application of images; we do not know his opinion on this subject.

But the scholarly world has never adopted an unchanging attitude toward Christian art; aside from the opinions we have already mentioned, there is another point of view. Thus an art historian, while basing himself on the same ancient writers as well as on St Justin and St Athenagoras, concludes: "The apologists say nothing about the Christians' opposition in principle to images; they only state that in their time there were very few images."[9] Indeed, had the Christians not allowed representations, we would not have discovered monuments of Christian art of the first centuries precisely in places where Christians assembled. On the other hand, the wide diffusion of images during the centuries that followed would be incomprehensible and inexplicable had they not existed earlier.

---

7 *Protrepticus* 4, *Clement of Alexandria*, trans. G. Butterworth (Cambridge: Harvard University Press, 1953), 133.
8 *Paedagogos*, PG 8: 633.
9 N. Pokrovskii, "Monuments of Christian Iconography and Art" (in Russian), 2nd ed. (St Petersburg, 1900), 16.

But there is another text which is invariably quoted to prove the Church's opposition to images. It must be admitted that it is more convincing than Clement's. This is canon 36 of the local council which took place in Elvira, in Spain, around the year 306: "It seemed good to us that paintings should not be found in churches and that that which is venerated and adored not be painted on the walls (*Placuit picturas in ecclesia esse non debere, nequod colitur et adoratur in parietibus depingatur*)." However, the meaning of this text is not as indisputable as is sometimes believed. Indeed, the reference is only to wall paintings, that is, to monumental decoration of the church building; other types of images are passed over in silence. We know that in Spain, at this time, there existed a large number of images on sacred vessels, on sarcophagi, and so forth. If the council does not mention them, this is because its decision may have been determined by practical reasons and not because it denied the sacred image on principle. Let us not forget that the Council of Elvira (the exact date of which is not known) was contemporary with the persecution of Diocletian. Should one not see in canon 36 rather an attempt to preserve "what is venerated and adored" from profanation: On the other hand, the aim of the Council of Elvira as a whole was to correct abuses in various domains. Could there not have been any in the veneration of images also?

What is decisive for the Church is not the antiquity of a given passage for or against the icon (the chronological factor), but the agreement or disagreement of this testimony with the Christian revelation.

The rejection of images in certain circles during the first Christian centuries may be explained by a certain confusion in the attitude toward the image—a confusion which was undoubtedly due to the lack of an adequate artistic and verbal language. To respond to all such ambiguities and to this diversity of attitudes toward art, one would have to discover art forms and verbal expressions that could not be misunderstood. In fact, the situation in the domain of art was the same as in theology or in the liturgy. Such lack of clarity and of unity is due to the creature's difficulty in accepting, assimilating and expressing that which transcends it. Moreover, the fact that Christ chose the Judaeo-Greco-Roman world for His Incarnation should also be taken into account. In that world, the reality of the Incarnation of God and the mystery of the cross were a scandal to some, folly to others. Scandal and folly were therefore in the image which reflected these, the icon. But the Christian *kerygma* was addressed precisely to this world. In order gradually to accustom the people to the inconceivable reality of the Incarnation, the Church first spoke to them in a language that was more readily accessible than a direct image. Therein, it seems, lies one of the main reasons for the abundance of symbols in the first Christian centuries. What was used, as St Paul says, was liquid nourishment, fit for childhood. The iconic quality of the image penetrated only slowly and with difficulty into the awareness of the people, and into their art. Only time and the needs of various historic epochs evinced this sacred character of the image, brought about the disappearance of the primitive symbols, and purified Christian art from all sorts of alien elements that concealed its content.

Thus, in spite of the fact that certain tendencies antagonistic to images existed within the Church, there was also, and above all, an essential trend favorable to images, one which became increasingly dominant without being formulated explicitly. It is this trend which is expressed by the Tradition of the Church when it speaks of the existence of the icon of the Lord when He lived on earth, and of icons of the Virgin made soon afterwards, precisely after Pentecost. This Tradition attests that within the Church there was from the beginning a clear understanding of the meaning and scope of the image, and that the attitude of the Church towards the image is invariably the same, since this attitude derives from its teaching on the Incarnation of God. This image therefore belongs to the very nature of Christianity, since it is not only the revelation of the Word of God, but also of the Image of God, manifested by the God-Man. The Church teaches that the image is based on the Incarnation of the second person of the Trinity. This is not a break with nor even a contradiction of the Old Testament, as the Protestants understand it; but, on the contrary, it clearly fulfills it, for the existence of the image in the New Testament is implied by its prohibition in the Old. Even though this may appear to be strange, the sacred image for the Church proceeds precisely from the *absence* of the image in the Old Testament. The forerunner of the Christian image is not the pagan idol, as is sometimes thought, but the absence of direct iconography before the Incarnation, just as the forerunner of the Church is not the pagan world, but the Israel of old, the people chosen by God to witness His revelation. The prohibition of the image which appears in Exodus (20:4) and in Deuteronomy (5:12–19) is a provisional, pedagogic measure which concerns only the Old Testament, and is not a prohibition in theory. "'Moreover I gave them statues that were not good' (Ez 20:25) because of their callousness," says St John of Damascus, explaining this prohibition[10] by means of a biblical quotation. Indeed, the prohibition of all direct and concrete images was accompanied by the divine commandment to establish certain symbolic images, those prefigurations which were the tabernacle and everything which it contained, and the smallest details of which were, so to speak, dictated by God.

The teaching of the Church on this subject is clearly explained by St John of Damascus (Fig. 2) in his three *Treatises in the Defense of Holy Icons*, written in response to the iconoclasts, who limited themselves to the biblical prohibition and confused the Christian image with the idol. Comparing the Old Testament texts and the Gospel, St John shows that the Christian image, far from contradicting the prohibition of the Old Testament, is, as we have said, its result and conclusion, since it arises from the very essence of Christianity.

His reasoning can be summarized as follows: in the Old Testament, God manifests Himself directly to His people only by sound, by word. He does not show Himself, and remains invisible. Israel does not see any image. In Deuteronomy (4:12), we read: "The Lord spoke to you out of the midst of the fire; you heard the sound of words, but saw no form; there was only a voice." And a bit further (4:15), we read: "Therefore take good heed to yourselves. Since you saw no form on the day that the Lord spoke to you at Horeb out of the midst of the fire." The prohibition comes immediately afterwards (4:16–19).

> Beware lest you act corruptly by making a graven image for yourselves, in the form of any figure, the likeness of male or female, the likeness of any beast that is on the earth, the likeness of any winged bird that flies in the air, the likeness of any thing that creeps on the ground, the likeness of any fish that is in the water under the earth. And beware lest you lift up your eyes to heaven, and when you see the sun and the moon and the stars, all the host of heaven, you be drawn away and worship them and serve them...

10 *De imaginibus oratio II*, ch. 15, PG 94: 1301C. For an English translation, see *St John of Damascus. On the Divine Images*, trans. David Anderson (New York: St Vladimir's Seminary Press, 1980).

2. *St John of Damascus*

Thus when God speaks of creatures, He forbids their representation. But when He speaks of Himself, He also forbids the making of His image, stressing the fact that He is invisible. Neither the people, nor even Moses saw any image of Him. They only heard His words. Not having seen God's image, they could not represent it; they could only write down His divine word, which is what Moses did. And how could they represent that which is incorporeal and indescribable, that which has neither shape nor limit? But in the very insistence of the biblical texts to emphasize that Israel *hears* the word but does not *see* the image, St John of Damascus discovers a mysterious sign of the future possibility of seeing and representing God coming in the flesh. "What is mysteriously indicated in these passages of Scripture?," he asks.

> It is clearly a prohibition against representing the invisible God. But when you see Him who has no body become man for you, then you will make representations of His human aspect. When the Invisible, having clothed Himself in the flesh, becomes visible, then represent the likeness of Him who has appeared... When He who, having been the consubstantial Image of the Father, emptied Himself by taking the form of a servant [Phil 2:6–7], thus becoming bound in quantity and quality, having taken on the carnal image, then paint and make visible to everyone Him who desired to become visible. Paint His birth from the Virgin, His baptism in the Jordan, His transfiguration on Mount Tabor... Paint everything with words and with colors, in books and on boards.[11]

Thus the very prohibition against representing the invisible God implies the necessity of representing God once the prophecies have been fulfilled. The words of the Lord, "You have seen no images; hence do not create any," mean "create no images of God *as long as you have not seen Him*." An image of an invisible God is impossible, "for how can that which is inaccessible to the eye be represented?"[12] If such an image were made, it would be based on imagination and would therefore be a falsehood and a lie.

One can therefore say that the scriptural prohibition against representing God is connected with the overall destiny of the Israelites. The purpose of the chosen people was to serve the true God. Theirs was a mission consisting in preparing and prefiguring that which was to be revealed in the New Testament. This is why there could only be symbolic

11 *Oratio I*, ch. 8, PG 94: 1237D–1240A, and *Oratio III*, ch. 8, PG 94: 1328D.
12 *Oratio III*, ch. 4, PG 94: 1321.

prefigurations, revelations of the future. "The law was not an image," says St John of Damascus, "but it was like a wall which hid the image." The Apostle Paul says: "The law was but a shadow of the good things to come instead of the true form of these realities" (Heb 10:1).[13] In other words, it is the New Testament which is the true image of reality.

But what about the prohibition against images of *creatures* given by God to Moses? This principle clearly has only one purpose: to forbid the chosen people to worship creatures in place of the Creator. "You shall not bow down to them or serve them" (Ex 20:5 and Dt 5:9). Indeed, given the leanings of the people towards idolatry, creatures and all images of creatures could easily be deified and worshiped. After the fall of Adam, man, together with the entire terrestrial world, became subject to corruption. This is why the image of man corrupted by sin or the image of terrestrial beings could not bring man closer to the only true God and could only lead him in the opposite direction, that is, to idolatry. This image was fundamentally impure.

In other words, the image of a creature cannot be a substitute for the image of God, which the people had not seen when the Lord spoke on Horeb. In the face of God, the creation of a substitute is always an iniquity. Hence these words: "Beware lest you act corruptly by making a graven image for yourselves, in the form of any figure, the likeness of any beast that is on the earth" (Dt 4:16).

But this prohibition is clearly a step to protect the specific ministry of the chosen people from corrupt practices. This clearly emerges from God's command to Moses to build, according to the image shown to him on the mountain, the tabernacle and all that it was to contain, including the gilded cherubim cast in metal (Ex 25:18; 26:1, 31). This commandment first of all signifies the possibility of expressing spiritual reality through art. Furthermore, it was not just a matter of representing cherubim in general or anywhere, since the Jews would have been able to come to idolize these images as easily as those of all other creatures. Cherubim could be represented only as servants of the true God in the tabernacle, in a place and posture appropriate to this honor.

This exception to the general rule shows that the prohibition of images

---

13 *Oratio I*, ch. 15, PG 94: 1244.

was not absolute. "Solomon, who received the gift of wisdom, when he made representations of the sky, made images of cherubim, lions and bulls," says St John of Damascus.[14] The fact that such creatures were represented near the temple, that is, where the only true God was worshiped, excluded any possibility of adoring them.[15]

To build the tabernacle according to the model shown on the mountain, God chose special men. It was not simply a matter of natural gifts and of the ability to follow Moses' instructions: "I have filled him [Bez'alel] with the Spirit of God, with ability and intelligence, with knowledge and all craftsmanship"; and further, speaking of all those who would work with Bez'alel: "I have given to all men ability, that they may make all that I have commanded you" (Ex 31:3 and 6). It is clearly shown here that art which serves God is not like any other art. It is based not only on the talent and wisdom of men, but also on the wisdom of the Spirit of God, on an intelligence granted by God Himself. In other words, divine inspiration is the very principle of liturgical art. Here the Scripture draws a line between liturgical art and art in general. This specific character and this divine inspiration are not only characteristic of the Old Testament, but also belong to the very principle of sacred art. This principle certainly remains valid in the New Testament.

But let us return to the explanations of St John of Damascus. If, in the Old Testament, the direct revelation of God was made manifest only by word, in the New Testament it is made manifest both by word and by image. The Invisible became visible, the Nonrepresentable became representable. Now God does not address man only by word and through the prophets. He shows Himself in the person of the incarnate Word. He "lives among men." In the Gospel according to St Matthew (13:16–17), says St John of Damascus, the Lord, the same Lord who spoke in the Old Testament, utters words honoring His disciples and all those who lived in their image and followed their footsteps:

Blessed are your eyes, for they see, and your ears, for they hear. Truly, I say to

14 *Oratio I*, ch. 20, PG 94: 1252.
15 It is interesting to note that if the ancient Hebrews did not forego (sculptured) images in the tabernacle and in Solomon's Temple, present-day Jews, by contrast, rigorously uphold the letter of the law and abstain from any sculptured image (see E. Namenyi, *L'esprit de l'art juif* [1957], 27).

you, many prophets and righteous men longed to see what you see, and did not
see it, and to hear what you hear, and did not hear it.[16]

It is obvious that when Christ says to His disciples that their eyes are
fortunate to see what they see and their ears to hear what they hear, He is
referring to that which has never been seen or heard, since men always had
eyes to see and ears to hear. These words of Christ also did not apply to
His miracles, since the prophets of the Old Testament also performed
miracles (Moses, Elijah, who resurrected a dead person, stopped the rain
from falling, etc.). These words mean that the disciples directly saw and
heard Him whose coming had been foretold by the prophets: the incarnate God. "No one has ever seen God," says St John the Evangelist, "the
only Son, who is in the bosom of the Father, He has made Him known"
(Jn 1:18).

Thus the distinctive trait of the New Testament is the direct connection between the word and the image. This is why the Fathers and the
councils, when speaking of the image, never forgot to stress: "That which
we have heard, we have seen. That which we have heard, we have seen in
the city of the all-powerful God, in the city of our God."[17] Henceforth,
what is seen cannot be separated from what is heard. What David heard
were prophetic words only, prefigurations of what has been realized in the
New Testament. At this moment, in the New Testament, man receives the
revelation of the Kingdom of God to come, and this revelation is given to
him by the word and the image—by the Son of God who became
incarnate Himself.

The apostles saw with their bodily eyes that which, in the Old Testament, was only foreshadowed by symbols: "God, who has neither body
nor form, was never represented in days of old. But now that He has come
in the flesh and has lived among men, I represent the visible appearance
of God."[18] Here lies the heart of the difference with the visions of the Old
Testament.

> I gaze upon the image of God, as Jacob did, but in a different way. For he only
> saw with spiritual sight what was promised to come in the future, while the
> memory of Him who became visible in the flesh is burned into my soul.[19]

16 *Oratio II*, ch. 20, PG 94: 1305–1308. Cf *Oratio III*, ch. 12, ibid., 1333.
17 Hebrew Bible, Ps 48:9.
18 *Oratio I*, ch. 16, PG 94: 1245.
19 *Oratio I*, ch. 22, PG 94: 1256A–B, trans. D. Anderson, *On the Divine Images*, 30–1.

At that time, the prophets saw with their spiritual eyes prefigurations revealing the future (Ezekiel, Jacob, Isaiah...). At present, man sees with his bodily eyes the realization of their revelations: the incarnate God. St John the Evangelist expresses this powerfully in the first words of his first Epistle: "That which was from the beginning, which we have heard, which we have seen with our eyes, which we have looked upon and touched with our hands."

St John of Damascus continues:

> Thus the apostles saw with their carnal eyes God who became man, Christ. They saw His passion, His miracles, and heard His words. And we too, following the steps of the apostles, ardently desire to see and to hear. The apostles saw Christ face to face because He was present corporeally. But we who do not see Him directly nor hear His words nevertheless listen to these words which are written in books and thus sanctify our hearing and, thereby, our soul. We consider ourselves fortunate, and we venerate the books through which we hear these sacred words and are sanctified. Similarly, through His image, we contemplate the physical appearance of Christ, His miracles and His passion. This contemplation sanctifies our sight and, thereby, our soul. We consider ourselves fortunate and we venerate this image by lifting ourselves, as far as possible, beyond this physical appearance to the contemplation of divine glory.[20]

Therefore, if we comprehend the spiritual through the words which we hear with our carnal ears, contemplation with our carnal eyes likewise leads us to spiritual contemplation.

This commentary of St John of Damascus does not express his personal opinion, or even a teaching that the Church has added, as it were, to its early doctrine. This teaching is an integral part of Christian doctrine itself. It is part of the very essence of Christianity, just as is the teaching about the two natures of Christ or the veneration of the Virgin. St John of Damascus only systematized and formulated in the eighth century that which existed from the beginning. He did so in response to a situation which demanded more clarity, just as he also systematized and formulated the general teaching of the Church in his work *On the Orthodox Faith.*

All of the prefigurations of the Old Testament announced the salvation to come, this salvation which is now realized and which the Fathers summarized in a particularly pregnant statement: "God became man so that man could become God." This redeeming act is therefore centered

---

20   *Oratio III*, ch. 12, PG 94: 1333, 1336.

on the person of Christ, God who became man, and, next to Him, on the first deified human being, the Virgin. On these two central figures converge all the writings of the Old Testament, expressed through human history, animals, or objects. Thus Isaac's sacrifice, the lamb, and the iron serpent prefigured Christ, and Esther, mediator of the people of God, the golden vase containing the divine bread, Aaron's staff, etc., prefigured the Virgin. The realization of these prophetic symbols is accomplished in the New Testament by the two essential images: that of our Lord, God who became man, and that of the Most Holy Mother of God, the first human being to attain deification. This is why the first icons, appearing simultaneously with Christianity, represent Christ and the Virgin. And the Church, asserting this by its Tradition, bases on these two images—the two poles of its belief—all its iconography.

The realization of this divine promise made to man also sanctifies and illumines creatures of the past, humanity of the Old Testament, by uniting it with redeemed humanity. Now, after the Incarnation, we can also speak of the prophets and the patriarchs of the Old Testament as witnesses of the humanity redeemed by the blood of the incarnate God. The images of these men, like those of the New Testament saints, can no longer lead us to idolatry, since we now perceive the image of God in man. According to St John of Damascus:

> We received from God the capability of judgment, and we know what can be represented and what cannot be expressed by representation. "So that the law was our custodian until Christ came, that we might be justified by faith. But now that faith has come, we are no longer under a custodian" [Gal 3:24–25; see also Gal 4:3].[21]

This means that we do not represent the vices of men; we do not make images to glorify demons. We make representations to glorify God and His saints, to encourage goodness, to avoid sin, and to save our souls.

The fundamental link between the image and Christianity is the source of the tradition according to which the Church, from the beginning, preached Christianity to the world in *both* word and image. This is precisely why the Fathers of the Seventh Ecumenical Council were able to say: "The tradition of making icons has existed from the time of the apostolic preaching."[22] This

---

21 *Oratio III*, ch. 8, PG 94: 1378.
22 Mansi XIII, 252B.

essential link between the image and Christianity explains why it appears in the Church and why silently, as a self-evident reality, it occupies the place that belongs to it, in spite of the Old Testament prohibition and some sporadic opposition.

3

The First Icons of Christ and the Virgin

The Tradition of the Church declares that the first icon of Christ appeared during His life on earth. This is the image which is called "the Holy Face" in the West; in the Orthodox Church it is called "the icon not made by human hands" (ἀχειροποίητος). The history of the provenance of this first image of Christ has been transmitted by texts of the liturgical service in its honor (August 16). Here, for example, is a sticheron in tone 8 from Vespers: "After making an image of Your most pure image, You sent it to the faithful Abgar, who desired to see You, who in Your divinity are invisible to the cherubim."[1] Another sticheron from Matins in tone 4 says: "You sent letters traced by Your divine hand to Abgar, who asked for salvation and health which come from the image of Your divine face." In general, and especially in the churches dedicated to the Holy Face, there are frequent allusions to the history of Abgar in the liturgical service of the feast. But they only mention the fact itself, without entering into detail.[2]

1   Abgar V Ukhama, Prince of Osroene, a small country between the Tigris and Euphrates, had as his capital the city of Edessa (now called Orfu or Rogaïs). Let us note in passing that the Chronicle of this city mentions the existence of a Christian church which was considered ancient in 1201, when it was destroyed by a flood. The kingdom of Edessa was the first state in the world to become a Christian state (between 170 and 214, under the rule of Abgar IX).

2   A more detailed version is found in the *Menaion* for the month of August. It is summarized as follows: King Abgar, a leper, had sent to Christ his archivist Hannan (Ananias) with a letter in which he asked Christ to come to Edessa to heal him. Hannan was a painter; and in case Christ refused to come, Abgar had advised Hannan to make a portrait of the Lord and bring it to him. Hannan found Christ surrounded by a large crowd; he climbed a rock from which he could see Him better. He tried to make His portrait but did not succeed "because of the indescribable glory of His face which was changing through grace." Seeing that Hannan wanted to make His portrait, Christ asked for some water, washed Himself, and wiped His face with a piece of linen on which His features remained fixed. He gave the linen to Hannan to carry it with a letter to the one who had sent him. In His letter, Christ refused to go to Edessa Himself, but promised Abgar to send him one of His disciples, once His mission had ended. Upon receiving the portrait, Abgar was cured of the most serious symptoms of his disease, though several marks remained on his face. After Pentecost, the apostle Thaddeus, one

Before the fifth century, ancient authors make no reference to the image of the Holy Face. The first time we hear it mentioned is in the fifth century, in a document called *The Doctrine of Addai*. Addai was a bishop of Edessa (d. 541) who, in his work (if it is authentic), undoubtedly used either a local tradition or documents about which we do not know. The most ancient undisputed author who mentions the icon sent to Abgar is Evagrius (sixth century); in his *Ecclesiastical History*[3] he calls the portrait "the icon made by God," Θεότευκτος εἰκών.

The original icon, i.e., the linen on which the face of the Lord is imprinted, was preserved in Edessa for a long time as the most precious treasure of the town. It was widely known and honored in the entire East; in the eighth century, Christians, following the example of the church of Edessa,[4] celebrated its feast in numerous places.

During the iconoclastic period, St John of Damascus mentions the miraculous image, and in 787 the Fathers of the Seventh Ecumenical Council refer to it many times. Leo, a reader of the Cathedral of St Sophia in Constantinople who was present at the Seventh Ecumenical Council, recounts how he himself venerated the Holy Face during his stay in Edessa.[5] In 944, the Byzantine emperors Constantine Porphyrogenitus and Romanus I bought the holy icon in Edessa. It was transported to Constantinople with great solemnity and placed in the church of the Virgin of Pharos. Emperor Constantine praised it in a sermon as the safeguard (*palladium*) of the empire. The liturgical service for the feast of

of the seventy, came to Edessa. He completely healed the king and converted him. Abgar had an idol removed from above one of the town gates and the holy image was placed there. But his great-grandson reverted to paganism and wanted to destroy it. The bishop of the town had it walled in, after having placed a burning lamp inside the niche. As time passed, the hiding place was forgotten, but it was rediscovered when Cosroes, king of the Persians, besieged the city in 544 or 545. The lamp was still burning. Not only was the image intact, but it had also been imprinted on the inner side of the tile which concealed it. In memory of this event, we now have two types of icons of the Holy Face: one where the face of the Savior is represented on a piece of linen, another where there is no linen, but where there is the Holy Face as it was imprinted on the tile, κεράμιον, in Russian *chrepie*. The only thing that is known about this icon on the tile is that it was found in Hierapolis (Mabbug), in Syria. Emperor Nicephorus Phocas (963–969) is said to have brought it to Constantinople in 965 or 968.

3   *Historia ecclesiastica* IV, 27, PG 86: 2745–2748.
4   Later on, in Edessa, beginning with the year 843, this feast coincided with that of the Triumph of Orthodoxy.
5   Mansi XIII, 169, 190ff. A. Grabar, "The Holy Face of the Cathedral of Laon" (in Russian), *Seminarium Kondakovianum* (Prague, 1930), 24.

the Transfer of the Holy Face to Constantinople, celebrated on August 16, probably dates back to this time, at least in part. After the sack of Constantinople by the Crusaders in 1204, all traces of this icon were lost.[6]

In France, there exists a famous icon of the Holy Face which is now preserved in the sacristy of the cathedral of Laon. Of Balkan, perhaps Serbian, origin, and dating back to the twelfth century, this icon was sent from Rome to France in 1249 by Jacobus Pantaleo Tricassinus, the future Pope Urban IV, to his sister, the abbess of the Cistercian Sisters of Monasteriolum (Montreuil-les-Dames, in the diocese of Laon).[7]

In its liturgical service, the feast of the Holy Face is called "The transfer from Edessa to the city of Constantine of the image of our Lord 'not made by human hands,' the image which is called the holy linen." The present-day Liturgy, however, does not limit itself to the mere remembrance of the transfer of the image from one place to the other. The essential point of this service is the dogmatic foundation of the image and its purpose.

The meaning of the expression "image not made by the hand of man" is to be understood in the light of Mk 14:38; this image is above all the Incarnate Word Himself who became visible in "the temple of his body" (Jn 2:21). From this moment on, the mosaic law that forbade images had no more meaning, and the icons of Christ became so many irrefutable witnesses to the Incarnation of God.[8] It is not an image created according to a human concept: it represents the true face of the Son of God who became man. According to the tradition of the Church, it derives from a

---

6   Here we are speaking only of the icons that are actually celebrated liturgically by the Church. But the historical sources mention several icons of the Holy Face which played an important role in the sixth and seventh centuries, especially during the Byzantine-Persian war. Some of them had replaced the labarum (see A. Grabar, *L'iconoclasme byzantin* [Paris, 1957], 30ff). In Georgia there is an icon of the Holy Face painted in wax that dates back to the sixth or seventh century (see Amiranachvili, *Istoriia gruzinskogo iskusstva* [Moscow, 1950], 126).

7   The fifteenth century saw the appearance of the legend of St Veronica, who is represented as holding a linen on which the Holy Face is imprinted. There are several versions of the story of St Veronica. The best known is the one usually seen in the "Stations of the Cross," introduced by the Franciscans (the Fourth Station): when Christ was being led to Golgotha, a woman named Veronica wiped His sweat with a piece of linen on which His image remained imprinted (on this subject, see the article by Paul Perdrizet in *Seminarium Kondakovianum*, 5 [Prague, 1932], 1–15).

8   See V. Lossky, "The Savior Acheiropoietos," in L. Ouspensky and V. Lossky, *The Meaning of Icons*, trans. G. E. H. Palmer and E. Kadloubovsky (New York: St Vladimir's Seminary Press, 1982), 69.

3. *Holy Face.* Wall-painting, Paris.
Icon painted by the monk Gregory Kroug
Holy Trinity Church. Vanves, Paris.

direct contact with His Face. It is this first image of God who became man
which the Church venerates on the day of the Holy Face (Fig. 3).

As we have seen, the stichera quoted above, together with the other
liturgical texts, emphasize the historical origin of the image. As always, the
Church brings us back to the historical reality, just as in the Creed the
Church speaks of the crucifixion "under Pontius Pilate." Christianity is
not concerned with a "universal Christ," a personification of the internal
spiritual life, nor with an abstract Christ, a symbol of some grand idea. It
is essentially concerned with a historical person who lived in a definite
place, at a precise time: "Having saved Adam," we hear in a sticheron of
the feast, "the Savior, indescribable in His essence, lived on earth among
men, visible and distinguishable" (second sticheron in tone 1 during
Little Vespers).

The scriptural readings of the day are of particular importance for our
study. All of these readings reveal the meaning of the event which is being
celebrated. They begin by bringing out the biblical prefigurations. By
exalting the realization of the event in the New Testament, they emphasize its eschatological dimension. The choice of texts reveals precisely
what we have already learned from the works of St John of Damascus, i.e.,
how the Church understands the Old Testament's prohibition of images
and the meaning and purpose of the New Testament image.

First of all, we have the three Old Testament readings (*paroimiai*) of
Vespers: two are taken from Deuteronomy (4:6–7, 9–15; and 5:1–7,
9–10, 23–26, 28; 6:1–5, 13, 18) and the last is an excerpt from 3 Kings
(1 Kings in the Hebrew Bible) 8:22–23 and 27–30.[9]

The first two readings speak of the revelation of the law to the people
of Israel on Mount Horeb just before the entry of the Chosen People into
the Promised Land. The meaning of the readings can thus be summarized
by the fact that, in order to enter into this Promised Land and to own it,
it is essential for the people to observe the revealed law and to adore the
only true God with undivided adoration, without any confusion with the
cult of other "gods." One is also reminded that it is impossible to
represent the invisible God: "You heard the sound of words, but saw no

---

9   We take the readings directly from the Bible and not from the *Menaion* where they are
    abridged, and some passages important for the meaning of the image are omitted.

form; there was only a voice," and "take good heed to yourselves, since you saw no form," etc. Therefore the law in its totality, and in particular the prohibition against adoring other "gods" and against making images, is an indispensable condition of entry into the Promised Land. And, of course, the Promised Land is a prefiguration: It is an image of the Church, of the Kingdom of God.

The third reading is also a prefiguration of the New Testament revelation. It includes the prayer of Solomon at the consecration of the temple which he had built: "But will God indeed dwell on the earth?," asks Solomon. "Behold, heaven and the highest heaven cannot contain Thee; how much less this house which I have built!" All this alludes to the future coming of God on earth, to His participation in the course of human history, to the presence in a terrestrial temple, built by man, of the One for whom "the highest heaven does not suffice."

The meaning of these Old Testament readings is more fully revealed in the Epistle reading at the Liturgy (Col 1:12–17):

> Giving thanks to the Father, who has qualified us to share in the inheritance of the saints in light. He has delivered us from the dominion of darkness and transferred us to the kingdom of his beloved Son, in whom we have redemption, the forgiveness of sins. He is the image of the invisible God, the first-born of all creation.

Thus the entire development of the Old Testament, which defended the purity of the Chosen People, the entire sacred history of Israel, appears as a providential and messianic process, as a preparation for the appearance of the Body of Christ on earth, the New Testament Church. And in this preparatory process, the prohibition of images leads to the appearance of the One who was invisible, to "the image of the invisible God" revealed by the God-Man Jesus Christ. As we hear in the Vigil of the feast: "In former times, Moses could obscurely contemplate the divine glory from behind; but the new Israel now sees Thee clearly face to face" (second troparion of the fourth ode of the canon).

Let us finally examine the Gospel readings for the day of the Holy Face, both at Matins and at the Liturgy (Lk 9:51–56; and 10:22–24):

> When the days drew near for Him to be received up, He set his face to go to Jerusalem. And He sent messengers ahead of Him, who went and entered a village of the Samaritans, to make ready for Him; but the people would not receive Him, because His face was set toward Jerusalem. And when His disciples

James and John saw it, they said, "Lord, do you want us to bid fire come down from heaven and consume them?" But He turned and rebuked them. And they went on to another village. And Christ turned to His disciples saying, "All things have been delivered to me by my Father; and no one knows who the Son is except the Father, and who the Father is except the Son and any one to whom the Son chooses to reveal Him." Then turning to the disciples, He said privately, "Blessed are the eyes which see what you see! For I tell you that many prophets and kings desired to see what you see, and did not see it, and to hear what you hear, and did not hear it."

As far as the image is concerned, we see that the meaning of the Epistle and of the Gospel is the opposite of that found in the first two readings. The Old Testament texts say: "You saw no divine form." In the Gospel we read: "Blessed are the eyes which see what you see," that is, "the image of the invisible God," Christ. This is why the last words of the Gospel readings are only addressed to the apostles. In fact, not only the disciples but all those who surrounded Him saw the man Jesus. But only the apostles discerned in this son of man, under His "form of a servant," the Son of God, "the brightness of the glory of the Father." As we have seen, St John of Damascus understands these last words of the Gospel as the repeal of the biblical prohibition, the repeal which for us is the visible aspect of the image of Christ whom we worship. "Formerly Thou wast seen by men," we hear in a troparion, "and now Thou appearest in Thy image not made by human hand" (second troparion of the first ode of the canon).

The first Gospel passage (Lk 9:55–56) draws a sharp distinction between the apostles and the world. In fact, it shows what makes *the Church different from the world*: the spirit and the ways which are the Church's alone and which are not the world's. (Remember that it is this difference which determines the Church's modes of action and, in particular, its art.) On the one hand, the Old Testament readings explain why images were prohibited. The Gospel, on the other hand, reveals the purpose of the image. Note also that this difference of the spirit and the ways of the apostles from those of the world is noted by Christ just before His entrance into Jerusalem. Starting with the Old Testament readings and moving to the New Testament readings, we see a developing revelation through symbolic images: The Old Testament is a preparation for the New Testament; the Promised Land is an image of the Church. The New

Testament is the realization of these preparatory prefigurations. But the New Testament itself is not yet the final end: It is only another step toward the Kingdom of God. Thus in the Old Testament the confession of the true God and the absence of His image were essential conditions for the people to be able to enter the Promised Land and to possess it. In turn, in the New Testament the confession of Christ and of His image, the declaration of our faith in this image, plays an analogous role: It is also an essential condition to enter the Church and, through the Church, the Kingdom of God, that celestial Jerusalem toward which the Church is leading us. This is why this passage of the Gospel is read precisely on the day when the Church celebrates the icon of the Holy Face. It is Christ Himself who leads His apostles into Jerusalem. As for us, it is His image which leads us into the celestial Jerusalem. A hymn of the feast proclaims: "We praise Thee, the lover of man, by gazing upon the image of Thy physical form. Through it, grant unto Thy servants, O Savior, to enter into Eden without hindrance" (sticheron in tone 6).

Thus, by its choice of liturgical readings, the Church unfolds an immense picture before us, showing the slow and laborious progress of the fallen world towards the promised redemption.

Thus, the Church maintains that authentic images of Christ have existed from the very beginning. We also have historical evidence for this. This attestation is all the more valuable since it comes from the only ancient writer who was incontestably iconoclastic, the church historian Eusebius, Bishop of Caesarea. Not only does he confirm the existence of Christian images, "He even holds that in his time there still existed true images of Christ and of the apostles; he says that he has seen these himself."[10] Indeed, after describing the famous statue erected by the woman with an issue of blood whose story we know from the Gospel (Mt 9:20–23; Mk 5:25–34; Lk 8:43–48), Eusebius continues:

This statue, they said, bore the likeness of Jesus. And it is in existence even to our day, so that we saw it with our own eyes when we stayed in the city. And there is nothing surprising in the fact that those heathen, who long ago had good deeds done to them by our Savior, should have made these objects, since we saw (ἱστορήσαμεν) *the likeness of His apostles also, of Paul and Peter, and indeed of Christ Himself,* preserved in pictures painted in colors. And this is what we should

10 Ch. von Schönborn, *L'Icône du Christ. Fondements théologiques* (Freiburg, 1976), 75.

4. *Vladimir Mother of God.* XVIth century.
(Eleousa type)
Photo: Temple Gallery, London

expect, for the ancients were wont, according to their pagan habit, to honor them as saviors, without reservation, in this fashion.[11]

Let us repeat that Eusebius can hardly be suspected of exaggerating, since the theological trend to which he belonged was not about to approve the facts which he states here.

If the icon of Christ, the basis for all Christian iconography, reproduces the traits of God who became man, the icon of the Mother of God, on the other hand, represents the first human being who realized the goal of the Incarnation: the deification of man. The Orthodox Church declares that the Virgin is linked to fallen mankind which bears the consequences of original sin; the Church did not exclude her from Adam's lineage. At the same time, her preeminent dignity as the Mother of God, her personal perfection, and the ultimate degree of holiness which she acquired, explain this entirely exceptional veneration: the Virgin is the first of all humanity to have attained, through the complete transfiguration of her being, that to which every creature is summoned. She has already transcended the boundary between time and eternity and now finds herself in the Kingdom which the Church awaits with the second coming of Christ. She who "contained the uncontainable God," "the true Mother of God" (*Theotokos*), according to the solemn proclamation of the Fourth Ecumenical Council (Ephesus 431), presides with Christ over the destiny of the world. Her image therefore occupies the first place after that of Christ, and matches it. It differs from the icons of other saints and angels both by the variety of iconographic types as by their quantity and the intensity of their veneration.[12]

Orthodox tradition attributes the first icon of the Virgin to St Luke the Evangelist who, it is said, painted three of them after Pentecost. One of these belongs to the type called "Umilenie" ('Ελεοῦσα) (Fig. 4), "Our Lady of Tenderness." It represents the mutual caress of Mother and Child, and emphasizes the natural human feeling, the tenderness of motherly love. It is the image of a Mother who suffers deeply for the anguish which

11 Eusebius of Caesarea, *Ecclesiastical History*, Bk VII, chap. 18, trans. J. E. L. Oulton (Cambridge: Harvard University Press, 1964), 177.

12 Let us note that the calendar of the Russian church, where the iconography of the Virgin is highly developed, mentions 260 of her icons noted for miracles and celebrated liturgically. As for the overall number of designations of icons of the Virgin, the *Menaion* of Sergius mentions 700 of them (*Annus ecclesiasticus graeco-slavicus*, 2nd ed. [1901], vol. 1).

5. *Smolensk Mother of God.* XVIth century.
(Hodigitria type)
Photo: Castle De Wijenburgh, Echteld

awaits her Son in silent consciousness of His inevitable sufferings. Another image is of the type called "Hodigitria" (ἡ Ὁδηγήτρια) (Fig. 5), "She who leads the way." Both the Virgin and the Child are represented full face, turned toward the viewer. This hieratic, majestic image particularly emphasizes the divinity of the child. As for the third icon, it represented, they say, the Virgin without the Child. The facts about it are confused. It is probable that this icon resembled the one of the Virgin in the Deisis, praying to Christ. Actually, a score of icons attributed to St Luke are found in the Russian church alone. Besides these, there are twenty-one on Mount Athos and in the West, of which eight are in Rome. Obviously, it cannot be maintained that these icons are themselves made by the hand of the Evangelist, since nothing which he painted has survived.[13] But the so-called "St Luke icons" have their place in a tradition for which he furnished the prototype. They were painted according to reproductions of St Luke's originals. Here the apostolic tradition should be understood as it is understood when one speaks of the "apostolic liturgy" or of the "apostolic canons." These date back to the apostles not because they were written by their hand, but because they have an apostolic character and are covered by apostolic authority. The same is true for the so-called "St Luke icons."

The tradition which attributes the first icons of the Virgin to St Luke is transmitted by liturgical texts, particularly those of the feasts consecrated to the Virgin, such as the feast of Our Lady of Vladimir, an icon of the *Umilenie* type (May 21, June 23, August 26). During Vespers, the following *sticheron* in tone 6 is sung during the *lite*:

When for the first time your icon was painted by the announcer of evangelical mysteries and was brought to you so that you could identify it and confer on it the power of saving those who venerate you, you rejoiced. You who are merciful and who have blessed us became, as it were, the mouth and the voice of the icon. Just as when you conceived God, you sang the hymn: "Now all the generations will call me blessed," so also, looking at the icon, you say with force: "My grace and my power are with this image." And we truly believe that you have said this,

13 Thus, among the ancient reproductions of the Virgin of the *Umilenie* type, we do not know of any that is older than the tenth century (in the royal church Kilissa—963–969; see V. N. Lazarev, *Istoria vizantiiskoi zhivopisi* vol. 1 [Moscow-Leningrad, 1947], 125). As for the *Hodigitria* type, those of its prototypes we know date back to the sixth century (*The Gospel of Rabula.* See N. P. Kondakov, *Ikonografiia Bogomateri* vol. 1 [Petrograd, 1915], 191–2).

our Sovereign Lady, and that you are with us through this image...

During Matins, the first hymn of the canon in praise of the Virgin, tone 4, is: "Painting your all-honorable image, the divine Luke, author of the Gospel of Christ, inspired by the divine voice, represented the Creator of all things in your arms." If this second text simply states that the first icon of the Virgin was made by St Luke, the first adds that the Virgin herself approved her image, and conferred on it her power and her grace. Now, the Church uses this same text for the feasts of different icons of the Virgin, all of which go back to the prototypes formerly made by St Luke. By this, the Church emphasizes that the power and grace of the Virgin are transmitted to all the images which reproduce (together with the symbols which are her own) the authentic traits of the Mother of God painted by St Luke.

The oldest historical evidence we have about the icons painted by St Luke dates back to the sixth century. It is attributed to Theodore, called "the Lector," a Byzantine historian in the first half of the century (around 530) and a reader in the church of St Sophia in Constantinople. Theodore speaks of an icon of the Virgin *Hodigitria* sent to Constantinople in the year 450, which was attributed to St Luke. It was sent from Jerusalem by the Empress Eudoxia, wife of Emperor Theodosius II, to her sister, Pulcheria.[14] St Andrew of Crete and St Germanus, Patriarch of Constantinople (715–730), also speak of an icon of the Virgin painted by St Luke, but which was found in Rome. St Germanus adds that the image was painted during the life of the Mother of God, and that it was sent to Rome to Theophilus, the same "excellent" Theophilus who is mentioned in the prologue of the Gospel of St Luke and in the Acts of the Apostles. Another tradition tells of an icon of the Virgin which, after having been painted by St Luke and blessed by the Mother of God, was sent to the same Theophilus, but to Antioch.

In any case, from the fourth century on, when Christianity became the religion of the state and there was no longer any danger in exposing sacred

14 N. P. Kondakov, *Ikonografiia Bogomateri* vol. 2 (Petrograd, 1915), 154. The well-known writing in defense of icons, addressed to Emperor Constantine Copronymus and often attributed to St John of Damascus, also speaks of an image of the Virgin painted by St Luke. According to modern scholarship, this writing is by an anonymous author and is composed of prayers by St John of Damascus, as well as those of St George of Cyprus and St John of Jerusalem (see G. Ostrogorsky, *Seminarium Kondakovianum* I [Prague, 1927], 46, and *Histoire de l'Etat byzantin* [Paris, 1956], 179, by the same author).

objects, the icon of Theophilus, which until then had remained hidden in Rome, became known to an ever-growing number of Christians. The icon itself, or a reproduction, was moved from a private house to a church. And, in 540, St Gregory I (590–604) carried the venerable icon of the Mother of God, "which is said to be the work of St Luke" (*quam dicunt a sancto Luca factam*), to the basilica of St Peter in a solemn procession and with the singing of litanies.

Other than the images painted by St Luke, tradition also tells us of an icon of the Virgin made in a miraculous way and not by the hand of man. This image is called "Our Lady of Lidda" and is celebrated on March 12.[15] The miraculous nature of its origin was undoubtedly the reason which led people to see in this image a type of image analogous to that of Christ ἀχειροποίητος, and which caused the story of its appearance to be integrated into the Liturgy of various icons of the Virgin, namely that of the Kazan Mother of God (celebrated on July 8 and October 22). In the eighth century, St Germanus, the future patriarch of Constantinople, passing through Lidda, had a reproduction made of it which he sent to Rome during the time of the iconoclastic controversy. After the defeat of iconoclasm, it was returned to Constantinople. From this time on the image of "Our Lady of Lidda" was also called "Our Lady of Rome" (celebrated on June 26).

---

15 See N. P. Kondakov, *Ikonografiia Bogomateri*, vol. 1 (Petrograd, 1915), 176–79. The oldest written evidence we have on this subject dates back to the eighth and ninth centuries: it consists of a passage attributed to St Andrew of Crete written about the year 726, of the synodal letter written by the three patriarchs of the East to Emperor Theophilus, an iconoclast, in 839, and of a work by George, called "the Monk," written in 886–887. Nothing definite is known about the fate of this image, except that it still existed in the ninth century (V. Dobschütz, *Christusbilder* [Leipzig, 1899–1909], 79–80).

4

The Art of the First Centuries

Most of the monuments of the sacred art of the first centuries, especially those in the eastern part of Christendom, were destroyed by the iconoclasts, and later by the Crusaders, or simply by time. What remains especially are the frescoes, particularly in Rome.[1] We therefore do not know what the first icons of Christ and of the Virgin were like. But the little that remains of primitive art leads us to surmise that the first images were not purely naturalistic portraits, but rather images of a completely new and specific Christian reality. V. N. Lazarev[2] writes:

> Linked to antiquty, primarily to its late, spiritualized forms, this art, from the first centuries of its existence, is charged with a whole series of new tasks. Christian art is far from being an art of antiquty, as is thought by certain writers (especially Siebel). The new subject matter of primitive Christian art was not a purely external fact. It reflected a new outlook, a new religion, a fundamentally different understanding of reality. Such subject matter could not adapt itself to the old forms of antiquty. It required a style which could best incarnate the Christian ideals and, thus, all the efforts of the Christian painters were directed towards elaborating this style.

And Lazarev, relying on the research of other scholars, emphasizes that, in the paintings of the catacombs, this new style has already developed its basic characteristics. With the help of this art, the Christians attempted to convey not only that which is visible to the human eyes, but also that which is invisible, i.e., the spiritual content of that which was being represented. To express its teaching, the primitive Church also used pagan

1   Though we must constantly refer to the Roman catacombs, this does not mean that there were no Christians, or Christian art, elsewhere. On the contrary, Christianity spread much faster in the East than in the West, so much so, that when St Constantine came to the throne, the Christians already formed more than fifty percent of the population in parts of the East, in contrast to twenty percent in Rome. But it is in the Roman catacombs that most of the Christian monuments of the first centuries were preserved. Outside of Rome, catacombs also existed in Naples, Egypt and Palestine.

2   *History of Byzantine Painting* vol. 1 (in Russian) (Moscow, 1947), 38.

symbols and certain subjects from Greek and Roman mythology. It also employed art forms of Greek and Roman antiquty, but it gave them a new content, thus changing the very forms which express it.

To say this differently: as is true for human creation as a whole, the formation of the Christian image is now determined by the transvaluation Christianity has brought to the world. With the appearance of the new humanity appears a new image corresponding to it. Christianity creates its own life style, its own world vision, its own "style" in art. In opposition to the conception of the world in antiquty and the pictorial art which conveyed it, another conception of art appeared, a new artistic vision that broke with the world vision upon which the art of antiquity had been founded. This decisive break was caused by life itself, by the need to assimilate the accepted revelation and to set it against the heresies which truncated this revelation in its fulness.

The art of the catacombs is above all an art that teaches the faith. Most of its subjects, symbolic as well as direct, correspond to sacred texts: those of the Old Testament and of the New, as well as liturgical and patristic texts.

Side by side with the fairly numerous direct representations,[3] the language of symbols was very widespread and played an important role in the Church during the first centuries. This symbolic language can be explained, first of all, by the necessity of expressing through art a reality which could not be expressed directly. Furthermore, the main Christian sacraments remained hidden from the catechumens until a certain point, according to a rule established by the Fathers and based on the Holy Scripture. St Cyril of Jerusalem (fourth century) mentions the symbolic expressions which must be used in teaching Christians, "since all are permitted to hear the Gospel, but the *glory* of the Good News belongs only to those who are close to Christ." This is why the Lord spoke in

3   Thus, beginning with the first and second centuries, a whole series of themes from the Old and New Testaments appears in the catacombs. In the first century, these consist of: the Good Shepherd, Noah in the Ark, Daniel in the lions' den, and the banquet scene. From the second century, we have many images from the New Testament: the Annunciation, the Nativity of Christ, His Baptism, and many other subjects. Paintings in the catacombs frequently deal with themes inspired by the Gospel of St John: The Resurrection of Lazarus (fifty-three times), the healing of the paralytic (twenty times), and so forth. Some date back to the second half of the second century (see *Irénikon*, no. 2 [1961], 244–6; review of F. M. Braun, *Jean le Théologien et son évangile dans l'Eglise ancienne* [Paris, 1959]).

parables to those who were not capable of hearing, and then explained these parables to His disciples when they were alone. "Indeed," St Cyril continues,

that which for the initiated is a splendor of glory is blinding for those who do not believe... One does not explain the mysterious teaching of the Father, Son and Holy Spirit to a pagan, and even to the catechumens we do not speak clearly of the mysteries, but we express many things in a veiled way, for example, by parables, so that the faithful who know can understand, and those who do not know will not suffer harm.[4]

Thus the meaning of the Christian symbols was revealed progressively to the catechumens as they were prepared for baptism. On the other hand, relations between the Christians and the outside world also required some type of coded language. It was not in the interest of Christians to divulge the sacred mysteries to the outside world, which was pagan and hostile.

The early Christians primarily used biblical symbols—the lamb, the ark, etc. But once pagans began entering the Church, these symbols were no longer sufficient since pagans frequently did not understand them. And so the Church adopted some pagan symbols capable of conveying certain aspects of its teaching. The Church gave these symbols a new meaning, purifying them so that they would recapture their primitive meaning. They were then used to express the salvation accomplished in the Incarnation.

Thus, to allow for a better understanding of its teaching by pagan converts, the Church used certain myths of antiquty which, to a certain extent, paralleled the Christian faith.

We will give only a few examples which will help us to understand the purpose of such art, its meaning and content, and thereby the purpose and meaning of church art in general.

Beside the rare direct images of Christ, we find a large number of symbolic representations, either painted in the catacombs (Fig. 6) or carved in low or high reliefs on sarcophagi. First among such representations in human form, we find the type of the good shepherd, which appeared already in the first century. We find several such representations of it in the Roman catacombs of Domitilla. This image is closely linked to that of the lamb. This is based on biblical texts: for example, the prophet Ezekiel (ch 34) and David (Ps 22) represent the world as a sheep pen, the

4 *Or.* 6, par. 29, PG 33: 589.

6. *Christ and the Samaritan woman.*
Fresco from the Roman Praetextatus catacomb (2nd century).

shepherd of which is God. Speaking of Himself, Christ summarizes this biblical image, "I am the good shepherd," He says (Jn 10:14), or "I have been sent...to the lost sheep of the house of Israel" (Mt 15:24). Christianity adopted this iconographic type and gave it a precise, dogmatic meaning: the Good Shepherd—God incarnate—takes upon Himself the lost sheep, that is, fallen human nature, humanity which He unites to His divine glory. It is the deeds of Christ and not His historical form which are explained in this scene. In no way can this image be likened to that of the adolescent Christ, called Emmanuel.

Another symbolic representation of Christ is borrowed from ancient mythology: the rather infrequent representation of Christ as Orpheus, with a lyre in His hand and surrounded by animals. This symbol is frequently found in the writings of Christian antiquty, starting with Clement of Alexandria. Just as Orpheus subdued the wild beasts with his lyre and charmed the mountains and trees, so did Christ attract men with His divine word and subdue the forces of nature. Even those subjects which at first appear to be mere decorations often have a hidden meaning, such as the vine which is often seen in the art of the first centuries. This is obviously a visible transposition of the words of Christ:

> As the branch cannot bear fruit by itself, unless it abides in the vine, neither can you, unless you abide in me. I am the vine, you are the branches. He who abides in me, and I in him, he it is that bears much fruit, for apart from me you can do nothing. (Jn 15:4–5)

These words and this image have both an ecclesiological and a sacramental significance. The vine and the branches represent Christ and the Church: "I am the vine, you are the branches."[5]

But the image of the vine is most frequently completed by that of the harvest or by that of the birds feeding on the grapes. In this case, the vine reminds Christians of the central sacrament, the Eucharist. "The vine gives the wine as the Word gave His blood," says Clement of Alexandria.[6] The grape-gatherers and the birds who eat the grapes represent the Christian souls feeding on the body and blood of Christ.

5 This is most obvious when the image is found on the dome of a church (for example, the chapel of El Baouit, fifth century): The vine is in the center, while the branches completely cover the dome. This follows the same principle as the classic decoration in our churches, which depicts Christ in the dome and the apostles surrounding Him.

6 *Paedag.* Bk. 1, ch. 5, PG 8: 634.

In the Old Testament, the vine was also a symbol of the Promised Land, as was shown by the bunch of grapes brought to Moses by those whom he had sent to Canaan. Hence in the New Testament it is also a symbol of paradise, the land promised to those who commune in the body and blood of Christ, i.e., to the members of the Church. The decorative vine continues to exist today in the sacred art of the Orthodox Church and has the same symbolic meaning.

One of the most widespread symbols in the first Christian centuries was the fish.[7] The very important role played by the fish in the accounts of the Gospel certainly contributed to the fact that this symbol was adopted by the Christians. Christ Himself used it. The lake, the boat, the fishermen, the net heavy with fish do not form the framework for so many biblical scenes simply by chance. Speaking to fishermen, He naturally used images that were familiar and understandable to them; summoning them to the apostolate, He called them "fishers of men" ("Follow me, and I will make you fishers of people," Mt 4:19; Mk 1:17). He compares the heavenly kingdom to a net filled with many different kinds of fish. The image of the fish is also used as a symbol of the heavenly good things (Mt 7:9–11, 13, 47–48; Lk 5:10). The images of the fisherman and the fish, representing the teacher and the convert, are fully understandable. But there were other reasons for the wide dissemination of this symbol in Christianity. The most important of these is the mysterious meaning of the five letters which make up the word ἰχθύς.[8] This image is found everywhere: in mural paintings, on sarcophagi, in funeral inscriptions, on various objects. Christians wore little fishes around their neck made of metal, stone or mother-of-pearl, with the inscription "May You save" or "Save."[9]

To the extraordinary prevalence of the graphic image of the fish corresponds an equally striking literary use of it in funeral inscriptions and among many Christian writers.[10] However, the value of this symbol

7   This symbol has also been borrowed from paganism. Among primitive peoples, the fish symbolized fertility. Among the Romans at the beginning of the present era, it became an erotic symbol.

8   The Greek word meaning "fish," ἰχθύς, contains five letters which are the initials of five words directly corresponding to Christ: Ἰησοῦς Χριστός Θεοῦ Ὑιός Σωτήρ, "Jesus Christ, Son of God, the Savior." As we have seen, these words express the faith in the divinity of Jesus Christ, and in His redeeming mission. Therefore, we have in the symbol of the fish a kind of ancient credal formula, condensed into one word.

9   Dom H. Leclercq, *Manuel d'Archéologie chrétienne*, vol. 2 (Paris, 1907), 467–8.

10   Tertullian, Clement of Alexandria, St Augustine (430 AD), St Jerome (420 AD), Origen,

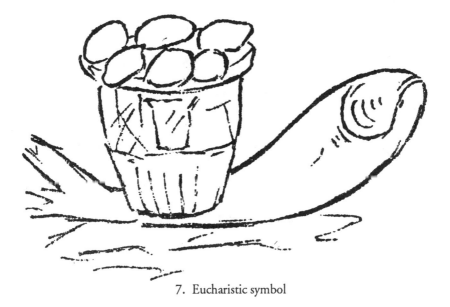

7. Eucharistic symbol

seemed so great to Christians of the first centuries, that they tried to hide its meaning for a longer time than for the other symbols, to such an extent that no writer gives a complete explanation of it until the fourth century, as far as we can judge from the available documents.

The first and essential meaning of the fish is therefore Jesus Christ himself. Some ancient authors occasionally call our Lord "the heavenly fish" (ἰχθὺς οὐράνιος). We find the image of a boat, symbol of the Church, carried by a fish: the Church rests on Christ, its founder. To represent Christ in the midst of Christians united to Him by baptism, little fishes surrounding a large one were portrayed. "We are little fish," Tertullian writes, "we are born in the water like our fish (ἰχθύς) Jesus Christ, and we can only be saved by staying in the water."[11] Thus the symbolism of the fish leads back to that of water, that is, to baptism.

What is particularly emphasized in the representations and writings which use the symbol of the fish is the eucharistic significance of this symbol (Fig. 7). Indeed, each time the Eucharist is represented, whether

Melito of Sardis, Optatus of Mileve (around 370 AD), St Zeno of Verona (around 375 AD), St Peter Chrysologus (450 AD), St Prosper of Aquitaine (463 AD) and many others used the symbolism of the fish.

11 See Sixte Scaglia, *Manuel d'Archéologie chrétienne* (Turin, 1916), 226.

as a banquet, a consecration scene or a simple symbol, the fish invariably appears. This is a fact. And yet, the fish has never been used as a eucharistic species. It only clarifies the meaning of the bread and wine. Of particular significance are two funeral inscriptions found at two different ends of the Christian world, in Phrygia and in Gaul, both dating back to the second century. The first is of St Abercius, Bishop of Hieropolis, who is venerated by the Church as "equal to the Apostles." This inscription reproduces a text written by the saint himself. A frequent traveler, he lived in Rome and throughout the East. "The faith led me everywhere," he writes. "Everywhere it fed me fresh, pure fish, caught by a holy virgin; it constantly fed this fish to friends; it has a delicious wine which it serves, mixed in water, with bread."[12] This fish, caught by the virgin, is Christ. The bread and the wine mixed with water already shows our eucharistic practice.

The other funeral inscription, found in France, is that of Pectorius of Autun. This is an acrostic poem in Greek in which the initial letters form the words ΙΧΘΥΣ ΕΛΠΙΣ, that is, "Jesus Christ, Son of God, Savior, Hope." In "the eternal waves of wisdom given by the treasures," in "the divine waters" which renew the soul, the "divine race of heavenly fish (ἰχθὺς οὐράνιος) receives...immortal life." Then the poem invites the reader to take soft nourishment, such as the honey of the Savior of the saints, and to eat the ἰχθύς "which you hold in the palm of your hand."[13]

Thus St Abercius saw everywhere, from Rome to the Euphrates, not only the same doctrine and the same sacrament, but also the same image, the same symbol in which rite and doctrine converge, that of the fish. The inscription of Pectorius speaks of the same reality at the other end of the Christian world, in Gaul. Thus, these two documents show us that the symbol of the fish was widespread and characteristic of the entire Church.

Another very widespread symbol of Christ in the catacombs is that of the lamb, which appears in the first century. We will have to return to this image when we discuss its suppression in the seventh century. It must only be mentioned that the lamb, like the fish, though primarily a symbol of Christ, could also represent the Christian in general, and the apostles in particular.

12 *Ibid.*, 248.
13 The custom of the first Christians was for the faithful to receive the consecrated bread in the palm of the right hand which was crossed over the left. This is how the Orthodox clergy receive Communion even today.

Lambs drinking from the streams represented the Christians drinking the water of life of the evangelical teaching. When there were two lambs, they represented the Church of the Jews and the Church of the Gentiles.

As the main symbol of Christ, the lamb appeared in place of the direct image of our Lord for a long time, even in historical scenes such as the transfiguration or baptism, in which not only Christ himself, but also the apostles or John the Baptist, were represented as lambs.

The Virgin is represented in the catacombs at least as often as Christ. But while Christ is primarily represented in symbols, the Virgin is always represented directly. As far as we can tell from what has been discovered up to now, she appears as early as the second century in various iconographic subjects, for example, the Annunciation (the catacomb of Priscilla) and the Nativity (the catacomb of St Sebastian, fourth century). She is also often represented alone, as an *Orans*, i.e., with arms lifted in prayer. This latter image emphasizes her role as the mediator before God for the Church and for the world. And it is usually in this pose that she is represented on the bottoms of many sacred vases (Fig. 8) in the catacombs. She also sometimes appears surrounded by the Apostles Peter and Paul and by others, or else with her mother, St Ann. One of the scenes in which she plays an important role is the Adoration of the Magi. Very frequently represented in the first Christian centuries, the Adoration of the Magi was a separate feast in the liturgical year, as is still the case in the Western confessions. In the Orthodox Church, it is included in the feast of the Nativity. In the Roman catacombs, ten or twelve images of the adoration of the Wise Men can be found, dating from the second to the fourth centuries. The Virgin is always represented sitting down, holding the Child on her lap and receiving with Him the adoration of the Wise Men, which particularly emphasizes her dignity as the Mother of God. This iconographic theme dealt with a very pressing question of that time, that of the role of the Gentiles, i.e., of the non-Jewish people in the Church. This no longer poses any problem for us, but in the first centuries, the problem of the Gentiles, of the pagans who entered the Church, the house of Israel for which Christ had come, was very acute. It was the source of a controversy among the Apostles (Acts 11:1–4) and was discussed at the apostolic council (Acts 15). It played an important role in the life of the first Christians (for example, Acts 6:1). Images frequently and in different ways reflected this problem. The Wise Men coming to adore Christ were the forerunners of the nations, the first-fruits of the Church of the Gentiles, i.e., of the non-Jewish Church. This is why the Christians of the first centuries, through the representation of the worship of the Wise Men, emphasized the place of the non-Jewish Christians in the Church, the legitimacy of their ministry parallel to that of the Christians of Israel.[14]

The images of Christ, direct or indirect, and those of the Virgin were followed by images of the apostles, prophets, martyrs, angels and so forth; in short, by the entire variety of Christian iconography.

A very distinctive example, which will help us understand the development of sacred art, is that of the oldest known representation of the Virgin and Child. It is a fresco in the catacomb of Priscilla (Fig. 9), a painting that is still entirely Hellenistic in style. To show that this woman with a child is the Virgin, one had to have recourse to external signs. These external indications include the representation of a biblical prophet beside her and of a star above her head. Here we see the same principle as in the images of the Eucharist already mentioned. Such a detail shifted the meaning of the image to an entirely different level: it illumined it with a salvific content. Similarly, to show that the woman represented with a child is not just any woman, but the Mother of God, the external signs—the prophet and the star—were necessary. Here, the prophet is holding a scroll or a little book containing the prophecy in his left hand, and is pointing to the star above the Virgin with his right hand. Is this Isaiah saying: "The Lord will be your everlasting light" (60:19)—indeed, the star is the symbol of the heavens and the celestial light—or is it Balaam who proclaimed: "A star shall come forth out of Jacob, and a scepter shall rise out of Israel" (Num 24:17)? The Virgin wears a veil on her head, the sign of a married woman. Her civil state was, indeed, that of a married woman, and this veil is a very important characteristic of historical realism which has remained a part of the Orthodox iconographic tradition. The picture is both a symbolic and a historical image.

14 Even in the sixth century, mosaics in the church of San Vitale in Ravenna represent the adoration of the Wise Men embroidered on the robe of the Empress Theodora, in that famous scene which shows her with Emperor Justinian, carrying gifts to the Church. Thus, the imperial couple reenacts the action of the kings of the Orient, carrying gifts to Christ in the name of their people.

8. Bottom of a vase from the catacomb of St Agnes representing
the Virgin in an *orans* position according to Garucci.

9. *Virgin and Child with a prophet.*
Fresco from the Priscilla catacomb (2nd century).

This union of historical truth and symbolism forms the basis of Christian sacred art. At this time, the artistic language of the Church, like its dogmatic language, did not as of yet have the accuracy, clarity and precision of the following centuries, which now permit us to recognize the Mother of God without a prophet pointing her out. The artistic language was in the process of being formed, and the frescoes in the catacombs illustrate well the first steps of this genesis.

In the art of the catacombs we find not only the very *principle* of sacred art, but also, its *external* character, at least in its general traits. As we have already said, secular, unprejudiced scholarship maintains that a new style, distinctive of Christianity, appeared already in the catacombs of the first centuries, a style which already possessed the essential traits that would henceforth characterize the art of the Church. Such art, we repeat, expresses above all the teaching of the Church and corresponds to sacred texts. Its aim, therefore, is not to reflect everyday life, but to throw the new light of the Gospel upon it. No traces can be found in the catacombs of images with a documentary, anecdotal or psychological character. It would be impossible, through this art, to provide a description of the everyday life of the early Christians. Thus, no trace of the frequent persecutions and the numerous martyrs of this time can be found in the liturgical art of the catacombs. The Christian artists who lived in the times of Nero or Diocletian undoubtedly saw the atrocious scenes in the amphitheaters, and these episodes were a matter of glory and consolation for all the brothers. One would expect to see recollections of these days when the struggle of the Christians against the pagan gods reached its climax. But not one scene of martyrdom can be found in the catacombs. The same holds true in the writings of the great saints of the time. St Paul, for example, teaches, denounces fallacies and vices, etc., but he mentions only in passing, without any allusion to his spiritual state and without any description, the tortures which he endured (2 Cor 11:23–27). It is therefore not surprising that we also find no evidence of these in art. It is only much later, when the persecutions had ceased and the anguish of the Christians had become history, that they were sometimes represented.

At the same time, such art was not cut off from life. It not only speaks the artistic language of its time, but is intimately connected with real life. This connection does not consist of episodic images like those in secular

10. *Daniel in the lion's den.*
Fresco from the Cimetero dei Giordani (4th century).

painting, but in the answer which it brings to the everyday problems of a Christian. The essential part of this answer is the state of prayer which this art communicates to the spectator. Seen face on or from the side, these persons are most often in the *orans* position, i.e., in the ancient position of prayer. Particularly widespread in the first centuries of Christianity, it gained a symbolic value. Thus many figures, appearing in this position and personifying either prayer or the Church, are seen in the Roman catacombs.[15] This

---

15 This position of uplifted hands is not an exclusively Christian pose; it was known in the world of antiquty and in the Old Testament, where the psalms refer to it many times.

state of prayer becomes the leitmotif of a wide variety of often dramatic situations, such as the sacrifice of Abraham, or Daniel in the lions' den (Fig. 10). The drama of the represented situation is not so much the very moment of sacrifice as the internal, spiritual state of the persons, i.e., the state of prayer. The Christian, who always had to be prepared to confess his faith through suffering, was therefore provided with an internal attitude which he had to preserve at all times. That which could calm, strengthen and teach was portrayed, and not that which could possibly repel or frighten. What these images also conveyed was the teaching of salvation. The sacrificed Isaac was saved, as were Noah and Daniel, and this portrayed our salvation. In addition to prayer, toil was also represented in order to demonstrate its purifying character and to remind Christians that all human toil should be to the glory of God. It was not some episode of human activity that was represented, but rather activity as such—occupations, for example. Thus we see a woman selling herbs at her stall, a ferryman loading or unloading a cargo of amphoras, dockhands unloading a ship, a baker, a wine-grower, a coachman, or coopers at work.

Another characteristic trait of Christian art, which can be seen already in the first centuries, is that the image is reduced to a minimum of details and to a maximum of expression. Such laconism, such frugality in methods, corresponds to the laconic and subdued character of Scripture. The Gospel dedicates only several lines to those events which decide the history of humanity. Similarly, the sacred image portrays only the essential. Details are tolerated only when they have some significance. All of these traits lead us directly to the classical style of the Orthodox icon. From this time on, the painter had to give great simplicity to his works, in which the profound meaning was understandable only to the eye initiated by the spirit. The artist had to purify his art of all individual elements; he remained anonymous (the works were never signed), and his first concern was to pass on tradition. Simultaneously, he had to renounce aesthetic joy for its own sake and use all the signs of the visible world in order to suggest spiritual reality. Indeed, to represent the invisible to the eyes of the flesh, a confused haze is unnecessary. On the contrary, one must be very clear and precise, just as the Fathers, who use particularly clear and vigorous expressions when they speak of the spiritual world.

The Christian painter renounces the naturalistic representation of space, so noticeable in the Roman art of this time. The Christian painter depicts neither depth nor shadows in his work. Instead of representing a scene which the viewer can only look at, but cannot participate in, he draws figures mutually bound to the general meaning of the image, and, above all, to the faithful who contemplate them. They are almost always represented face on, as we have already said. They address the viewer and communicate their inner state to him, a state of prayer. What is important is not so much the action that is represented, but this communion with the viewer.

As can be seen, the symbolism of this epoch is therefore not a more or less abstract, fanciful game of words. In it we discover a coherent and profound system of expression, penetrated in its entirety and in every detail by a unique message of mystery and of salvation. And this language fulfilled its task well, for it taught Christianity to thousands, educating and guiding them in the faith. It is precisely with the help of this now incomprehensible language that the saints of that time received their religious instruction, at each stage, from conversion to the crowning of their witness through martyrdom.

As we see in the first centuries of Christianity, the subjects represented were primarily either pure symbols, such as the fish or the vine, or historical images which also served as symbols—for example, the resurrection of Lazarus, an image of the general resurrection to come. As forms of expression, all symbols of this kind, once found and adopted by the entire Church, were no longer modified and were used in the whole Christian world. They became part of a common symbolic language, accessible and understandable to every Christian, irrespective of nationality or culture.

From the great number of monuments of early Christian art, we have taken only a few examples. They show us extremely well-developed methods of preaching and of religious initiation. The art of the first Christians was a doctrinal and a liturgical art. It embodied a true spiritual direction, and the claim of certain scholars who maintain that sacred art was born outside the Church, or that it had no importance until the third or fourth centuries, cannot be taken seriously.[16] Quite the opposite is true. This art

16 See, for example, M. Ochse, *La nouvelle querelle des images* (Paris, 1952), 41; or also Th. Klauser, "Die Äusserungen der alten Kirche zur Kunst," *Gesammelte Arbeiten zur Liturgie-Geschichte* (Münster, 1974), 336–7.

reflects a general ecclesiastical guidance and a tight control over the artists' work. Nothing was left to chance or to the whim of the artist. Everything is concentrated on the expression of the Church's teaching. From its first steps, the Church begins to develop an artistic language which expresses the same truth as the sacred word. We shall see later that this language, just like the theological expression of the Christian teaching, will become more and more specific throughout the Church's history, and will become a most perfect and exact instrument of teaching.

The beauty of this art of the first Christian centuries consists above all in the possibilities it conceals: its full meaning is not yet realized, but it promises an endless development.

However, the art of the Roman catacombs should not make us forget that what we deal with is only one branch of early Christian art, the Greco-Roman, which has been better preserved. The typical trait of the Greco-Roman art of this epoch is its naturalism, that is, its tendency to duplicate exactly nature or visible objects. The examples we have used demonstrate to what extent Christian art was breaking away from the principles of Greco-Roman art. The technique used in Greco-Roman art was very developed and highly perfected, and Christian art inherited this perfection. This is why the Christian art of the first and second centuries is characterized by the same freshness and spontaneity which distinguish the art of antiquty.

Besides this Greco-Roman branch of Christian art, there were others. Thus, the third-century frescoes in a Christian Church at Dura-Europos have a clearly Oriental character, the essential traits of which are delineated by Grabar in his description of a pagan temple in this same town:

> We find flattened figures with strongly marked outlines, isocephaly [all heads on a level], bodies without weight or substance, space reduced to a minimum, figures turning their heads towards the spectator as they move past—in a word, an expressive art that does not seek to imitate what the eye sees or give the illusion of material reality.[17]

These traits of Oriental art were frequently used by Christianity. Several other monuments and certain indicators lead us to the conclusion that sacred art was no less developed in the eastern part of the Empire than in the western. In any case, when Constantinople was founded in 330, Christian art in Rome and in the East already had a long history.

17 A. Grabar, *Byzantine Painting*, trans. Stuart Gilbert (Lausanne: Skira, 1953), 38.

5

Sacred Art in the Constantinian Epoch

In the fourth century, with the advent of the Constantinian era, a new period begins for the Church. The Church leaves its forced confinement and opens its doors wide to the world of antiquity. The influx of new converts requires larger places of worship and a new kind of teaching, one that is more direct and more explicit. The symbols used in the first centuries, intended for a small number of initiates, were incomprehensible to the new converts. This is the obvious reason why large historical cycles of monumental paintings portraying the events of the Old and New Testaments appeared in churches in the fourth and fifth centuries. St Constantine built churches in Palestine on the very sites where the biblical events had occurred. It is also in this period that the dates of most of the major feasts were set, along with the iconographic schemes for them, which are still followed in the Orthodox Church today. In any case, the series was complete in the sixth century, as it can be found on the famous phials of Monza (not far from Milan) (Fig. 11) and of Bobbio. These silver phials, decorated with scenes from the Gospels, were offered to Theodelinda, Queen of the Lombards (d. 625), around the year 600. They are for us a very precious document. Some scholars today agree in recognizing on these phials reproductions of mosaics of Palestinian churches built by Constantine and Helen. Other experts are more prudent: "It is more reasonable to say," A. Grabar states, "that their more remote models escape us at this time."[1]

Dating to the period between the fourth and sixth centuries, these phials are of considerable importance, because they offer us representations of several feasts, thereby confirming the antiquity of our iconography of these feasts. Indeed, some of them show a fully-developed iconography, the very same used today in Orthodox icons.[2]

1   A. Grabar, *Les Ampoules de Terre Sainte* (Paris, 1958), 49.
2   One of these phials even carries seven representations: those of the Annunciation, of the Visitation, the Nativity of Christ, His Baptism, the Crucifixion, the myrrh-bearing women at the tomb, and the Ascension.

11. A phial of Monza.

The change which occurred in the fourth century was not only external; this triumphant epoch was also one of great temptations and ordeals. The world which entered the Church brought with it all its restlessness and all its doubts, which the Church had to appease and to solve. The new contact between the Church and the world is characterized both by a flare-up of heresies and by a new vigor in Christian life. If, until this time, it had been the martyrs who were the pillars of the Church, now it was above all the theologians and the ascetic saints. This is a time of great saints, including St Basil the Great, St Gregory the Theologian, St John Chrysostom, St Gregory of Nyssa, St Anthony the Great, St Macarius of Egypt, St Mark, St Isaiah and many others. The empire became Christian, the world was gradually sacralized. But it is precisely this world on its way to sacralization, the Christian empire, which was to go to the desert. The people were attracted to the desert not because it was easier to live there, not because they wanted to flee from the difficulties of the world, but, on the contrary, because they wanted to escape the well-being of the world, the glamour of a society which only pretended to be Christian. By the end of the fourth century, all of Egypt is covered with monasteries, where the monks can be counted in the thousands. Pilgrims flock from everywhere, both from Asia and from the West. The experience of the ascetic Fathers and their writings spreads throughout the Christian world. From this time on, the theory and practice (*praxis*) of theology, that is, the teaching of the Church and the living experience of the ascetics, become the sources that feed sacred art, guide and inspire it. This art finds it necessary, on the one hand, to transmit truths that are formulated dogmatically, and on the other hand to communicate the living experience of these truths—the spiritual experience of the saints, the living Christianity in which dogma and life are one. All this has to be transmitted no longer to limited groups, but to the mass of believers. This is why the Fathers of this time attach great importance to the pedagogic role of art. In the fourth century, a golden age of theology, a great number of first-rate Christian authors make reference to the image[3] in their argumentation— as to a very important reality, the function of which is considerable. Thus, St Basil considers that painting possesses a greater power of conviction than his own words. After having uttered an entire oration in memory of the martyr St Barlaam, he finishes by saying that he does not want to humiliate the great martyr by his words, but that he yields his place to a higher language, to the "resounding trumpets of the masters." "Rise now before me," he says,

> you, painters of the saints' merits. Complete with your art this incomplete image of a great leader [i.e., the martyr Barlaam]. Illuminate with the flowers of your wisdom the indistinct image which I have drawn of the crowned martyr. Let my words be surpassed by your painting of the heroic deeds of the martyr. I will be glad to acknowledge such a victory over myself... I will look at this fighter represented in a more living way on your paintings. Let the demons cry, defeated once again by the courage of the martyr. Let them be shown once more the burned, victorious hand. And let the initiator of combats, Christ, also be represented in this painting.[4]

In his Oration on the feast of St Theodore, St Gregory of Nyssa explains that

---

3 St Basil the Great, St Gregory the Theologian (*Second Oration on the Son*), St John Chrysostom (*Third Oration on the Epistle to the Colossians*), St Gregory of Nyssa (*Oration on the Divinity of the Son and the Holy Spirit; Oration on the Martyr St Theodore*), St Cyril of Alexandria (*Oration to Emperor Theodosius*), and others.

4 *Homilia* 17, PG 31: 489AC.

the painter... having represented the great deeds of the martyr on this icon... and the image of the initiator of combats, Christ, has clearly recorded through the colors of art, the struggles of the martyr, as in a book... For the silent painting speaks on the walls, and does much good.[5]

Among western authors, St Paulinus, Bishop of Nola (353?-431?), wrote particularly detailed accounts of images. He built many churches and decorated them with sacred images which he describes at length in his letters and poems. A very experienced pastor, St Paulinus saw that images attracted the attention of Christians, and particularly of neophytes and catechumens, much more than did books. This is why he strove to have many images in his churches.[6]

In the fifth century, we have a similar characteristic indicated in the works of one of the greatest ascetic writers of antiquity, St Nilus of Sinai (d. 430 or 450), disciple of St John Chrysostom. A certain prefect, Olympiodorus, after having built a church, wanted to represent on the walls of one side of the large nave the earth with hunting scenes and a multitude of animals, and on the other wall fishing scenes. His primary concern, as he expressed it, was to preserve a full aesthetic quality. Olympiodorus asked St Nilus for his advice, and St Nilus writes:

My answer to your letter is that it is infantile and dangerous to seduce the eye of the faithful with such things... Let the hand of the best painter cover both sides of the church with images from the Old and New Testaments, so that those who do not know the alphabet and cannot read the Holy Scriptures will remember, while looking at the painted representations, the courageous deeds of those who served God without malice. Thus, they will be encouraged to emulate the ever-memorable virtues of these servants of God who preferred the heavens to the earth, and the invisible to the visible.[7]

Thus, the Church endeavored to lead all the senses, including sight, to a knowledge and a glorification of God. Indeed, sight has always been of great importance in the preaching of the Christian revelation. "Among our senses, sight is the one that has the most efficient power to perceive sensible reality," said St Basil the Great.[8] The concept of the priority of sight is shown very clearly in patristic writings (for example, those of St Athanasius the Great, St Gregory of Nyssa, and others). "The contempla-

5   De S. Theodore martyre, PG 46: 737.
6   Epistola 32, ad Severum, PG 61: 339.
7   PG 79: 577.
8   St Basil the Great, Comment. in Isaiam prophetam, ch. 1, PG 30: 132A.

tion of the visible Word," a contemporary author writes, "does not lead to passivity precisely because it is contemplation *of the Word*, and not an aesthetic emotion or the contemplation of an idea."[9] During this age, as later, faith was professed by demonstration.

> I ask you, man, if a gentile were to come to you and ask, "show me your faith, that I may believe," what would you show him? Would you not lead him from sensory realities to the invisible?... You lead him to a church...; you show him the holy icons.[10]

Much later, in Russia, the saintly prince Andrew of Bogolubov did not act any differently. When heterodox strangers had arrived, he said to his servants, "Have them enter the church and the gallery, so that they may see true Christianity and be baptized."[11]

Thus, at all times, the Church assigned great importance to the image. But it is not its artistic or aesthetic value which is praised, but its teaching value. The image is a true confession of the Christian faith. This dogmatic character is an essential trait of Orthodox sacred art throughout history. Beginning with the fourth century, however, we also have examples of the Church using the image, not only to teach, but also to fight heresy. In its struggle for the purity of its life and teaching, the Church, at the Council of Laodicea (around 343), confirmed Apostolic Canon 85, which deals with the sacred books, and put an end to improvisation in worship (canons 59 and 60), through which errors had crept into the liturgy. It is understandable that the Church also became more exacting in the field of art. To errors and heresies, it responded not only with the teaching of the Fathers, not only with the experience of the saints, but also with the liturgy and with images. In the image, it is sometimes the details, sometimes whole cycles of wall paintings or mosaics, which define the sound doctrine of the Church in opposition to heresies. It is particularly in response to the teaching of Arius, who saw Christ not as God but as a creature, a teaching which was condemned by the First Ecumenical Council (325), that the letters alpha and omega (A, Ω) are placed at the two sides of the image of Christ—an allusion to the words of the Apocalypse: "I am alpha and omega, the first and the last, the beginning and the

9   J. Ph. Ramseyer, *La Parole et l'Image* (Neuchâtel, 1963), 18.
10 *Adversus Constantinum Cabalinum,* par. 10, PG 95: 325.
11 *Complete Collection of Russian Chronicles* (in Russian), 591. Cited in particular by N. N. Voronin, *The Architecture of Northeast Russia,* vol. 1 (in Russian) (Moscow, 1961), 228.

end" (22:13)—in order more strongly to emphasize the divinity of the Son consubstantial to God the Father, according to the dogma of the Council of Nicaea.[12] In 431, the Council of Ephesus condemned the doctrine of Nestorius, who had rejected the hypostatic union of the divine and human natures in Christ, and who, consequently, had denied the divine motherhood of the Virgin, calling her Mother of Jesus or the Mother of Christ. The Council proclaimed the divine motherhood of the Virgin, solemnly attributing to Her the name of Mother of God (*Theotokos*). From then on, particularly solemn representations of the Virgin, sitting on a throne with the divine Child on her lap and with angels at her side, appeared everywhere.[13]

The task of developing the most appropriate forms of sacred art, its most precise pictorial language, fell on the Church of Constantinople. The geographical location of the new capital was particularly favorable: situated at the junction of Europe and Asia, it formed a bridge between them, and received a rich heritage from the one and from the other. In the realm of art, it adopted an already existing iconography of both the Old and the New Testaments, a perfected technique of fresco, of the mosaic and of the encaustic, a rich ornamentation, refined colors and a developed system of monumental decoration.[14]

To develop its language, the Church used, as we have seen, forms, symbols and even myths of antiquity, i.e., pagan forms of expression. But it did not use these forms without purifying them and adapting them to its own goals. Christianity absorbs everything that can serve as a form of expression from the world around it. Thus the Fathers of the Church used all the apparatus of ancient philosophy for the benefit of theology. Similarly, Christian art inherits the best traditions of antiquity. It absorbs elements of Greek, Egyptian, Syrian, Roman and other arts, sacralizing this complex heritage, guiding it in expressing the fullness of its own meaning and transforming it in accordance with the requirements of Christian teaching.[15] Christianity selects from pagan culture all that is its

12 L. Bréhier, *L'Art chrétien* (Paris, 1928), 67.

13 V. N. Lazarev, *History of Byzantine Painting* (in Russian) (Moscow, 1947), 51.

14 Recent archaeological discoveries have shown that Constantinople, from the beginning of its existence, was a very important center of artistic culture (see D. Talbot Rice, "Les mosaïques du grand palais des empereurs byzantins à Constantinople," in *Revue des Arts*, no 3 [Paris, 1955], 166).

15 The origins of Christian art are complex and no single factor can provide an exhaustive

own, all that was "Christian before Christ," all the truth which was expressed in it, and integrates this into the fullness of revelation.

According to the Fathers, the very name "Church" (ἐκκλησία) signifies a calling together, an assembly of all people in communion with God. Thus the people who are called from the world into the Church bring with them their culture, their characteristic national traits and their creative abilities. The Church then chooses from this contribution all that is purest, truest and most expressive and creates its sacred language. The first Christians had a eucharistic prayer which was very characteristic of this process: "As this bread, which at one time was scattered over the hills, has now become one, let Thy Church similarly be gathered from all the corners of the world into Thy Kingdom." This process of integration by the Church of those elements of the pagan world which are able to be Christianized is not a penetration of pagan customs into Christianity, but their sacralization. In the realm of art, this is not a paganization of Christian art and, therefore, of Christianity itself, as is often thought; but on the contrary, it is the Christianization of pagan art.

In this formative period of sacred art, there were two essential artistic trends, the roles of which were decisive. There was Hellenistic art, which represented the Greek spirit in Christian art, and the art of Jerusalem and of the Syrian regions. The use of these two highly contrasting trends illustrates well the selection process by which the Church elaborated the most adequate forms of its art. The Hellenistic trend was that of the Greek cities, particularly Alexandria. It had inherited the beauty of antiquity with its harmony, moderation, grace, rhythm and elegance. On the other hand, the art of Jerusalem and Syria represented historical realism, sometimes even a bit naturalistic and brutal (as, for example, in the Gospel of Rabula). The Church adopted from each of these art forms that which was most authentic. It discarded the sometimes coarse naturalism of Syrian art, but retained its truthful iconography, faithfully preserved in

explanation. For example, the icon is sometimes connected with the Egyptian funeral portrait because of the obvious resemblance between the two. Like the icon, the portrait presents the characteristic fixity of the face, but does not go beyond the life on earth. It aims at a kind of preservation which is reminiscent of Egyptian mummification. It tries to represent man as he was, as if he were still alive, and to preserve this image of life on earth for eternity. In an icon, on the contrary, the face is transfigured, and this very transfiguration reveals another world to us, a fullness incomparable to the fallen life. The Egyptian funeral portrait strives to prolong terrestrial life indefinitely, while the icon strives to deify it.

the very places where the biblical stories took place. From Hellenistic art, on the other hand, it rejected the somewhat idealistic aspects of iconography, but retained the harmonious beauty, the rhythmic feeling and certain other artistic elements, such as, for example, the "reverse" perspective. It rejects the Hellenistic iconography which portrays Christ as a young, god-like Apollo, beardless and elegant. It adopted the Palestinian iconography of a man with a dark beard, long hair, with realistic traits and great majesty. The same holds true for the Virgin. Hellenistic art gave the Virgin a tunic, a head-dress, sometimes even earrings like those worn by the grand ladies of Alexandria and Rome. The art of Jerusalem enveloped her in the long veil of Syrian women, a cloak which hid her hair and fell to her knees, just as we continue to represent her on our icons. The Church also uses the rhythmic and frequently symmetrical embellishments coming from the East, and other elements of different cultures which converged in Constantinople. With this large variety of elements, the Church of Constantinople created an art form which, already from the time of Justinian in the sixth century, was a well-developed artistic language.

The Church's acceptance of a variety of cultural elements and their integration into the fullness of revelation does not respond to a need of the Church but to a need of the world. The final goal of the world's existence is to become God's Kingdom. And, conversely, the purpose of the Church is to make the world participate in the fullness of revelation. This is why the process of selecting and assembling, which began in the first centuries of Christianity, corresponds to the normal saving task entrusted to the Church. This process is not limited to a specific historical period. It is a general trait of the role of the Church in the history of the world. The Church continues and will continue, until the consummation of the ages, to collect all authentic realities outside of itself, even those which are incomplete and imperfect, in order to integrate them into the fullness of the revelation, and to allow them to participate in divine life.

This does not mean that the Church suppresses the specific character of the cultural elements which it adopts. It excludes nothing which is a part of the nature created by God, not one human trait, not one indication of time and place, not one national or personal characteristic. It sanctifies all the diversity of the universe, revealing to it its true meaning, orienting it towards its true end: the building up of the Kingdom of God. Cultural diversity does not violate the unity of the Church, but offers it new forms of expression. Thus the catholicity of the Church is confirmed both in cultural wholeness and in the individual details. In the realm of art, just as in other areas, catholicity does not mean uniformity, but rather the expression of the one truth in a variety of forms, characteristic of every people, of every epoch, of every human being.

The art which was being developed was a manifestation of the new life which had been brought by Christianity, a life which was no longer subject to the law. According to the Christian apologist who wrote to Diognetus, Christians live "in the flesh," but they do not live "after the flesh."[16] Such words vividly express the very principle of the Christian life, and they do so in almost the same words used by St Paul in his letter to the Romans: "Therefore, brethren, we are debtors, not to the flesh, to live after the flesh" (8:12). But the world around the Church lived precisely *according to* the flesh, according to a principle directly opposed to Christian salvation. This idea of a triumphant flesh was expressed with great perfection in pagan art, this art of antiquity whose beauty retains its enticing charm even today. Christian art, meanwhile, had to reflect the principles of the specifically Christian life and to set them against the pagan life-style and its principles. The very meaning of Christianity demanded it.

The official art of the Roman empire was a state art which had to educate the citizens in a certain way. But this art of the Roman empire was a demonic art. The state was pagan and every official act was simultaneously a ritual act, a confession of paganism. When the Roman empire became Christian, the state was "depaganized," and its official art ceased to be idolatrous. Nonetheless, it remained a programmatic, pedagogical art. Whether Roman or Byzantine, this art was very different from secular art as we understand it today.

Life as it was, or rather as it was seen by the artist, was hardly represented. Even less could such art be called "free art" or "art for art's sake." It was not arbitrary: it was an educational art, expressing civic concepts, and educating the citizens in a clearly defined way.[17] To achieve

---

16 *The Epistle to Diognetus*, V, 8, trans. K. Lake, *The Apostolic Fathers*, vol. 2 (Cambridge, 1959), 361.

17 Furthermore, it is to this end that the artist often appealed to Christian elements. Thus, in

this, art was not limited to the representation of certain subjects; it did this in a clear and concise manner, calculated to make the subject-matter as accessible to the viewer and as readily digestible as possible. Each of its subjects had its own intention, its "function," so to speak.[18]

For the Church in its own domain, the spiritual, it was a question of possessing an art that would educate the Christian people in the same way the liturgy did, that would convey to them dogmatic teaching, and sanctify them with the presence of the grace of the Holy Spirit. In a word, what was needed was an art that would reflect the Kingdom of God on earth and accompany the faithful throughout their life, like a parcel of the Church in the world. What was essential was an image that would bring to the world the same *kerygma* as the word and the real presence of sanctification. By the sixth century, this artistic language already exists in its essential traits. This is the beginning of the art which will later improperly be called "Byzantine," or "in the Byzantine style," a term that would be arbitrarily extended to the art of all Orthodox populations.

order to show that imperial power was given by God, the emperor and empress were represented as crowned by Christ.

18 Thus the portrait of the emperor presented by a state official meant that this official was acting in the name of and with the power of the emperor; the image of the emperor trampling down a barbarian signified the invincibility of the empire, etc.

6

The Quinisext Council:
Its Teachings on the Sacred Image

As is true for the image itself, the teaching of the Church concerning icons is not an afterthought, a mere appendix to Christianity; it derives from the Christian teaching on salvation. The image was not at a given time put side by side to the Christian vision of the world: it has always been rooted at its very heart. From the beginning, it existed with an implicit fullness. As it did for other aspects of its teaching, the Church limited itself to making it more explicit in response to attacks and confusions that arose during the course of history. This is also true, for example, for the dogma of the two natures of Christ, the divine and the human. This truth was lived by the first Christians rather than explicitly formulated. The dogma's closely reasoned expression was created by the Church only in response to the demands of its history, to refute heresies and errors. It is at the Quinisext Council that the Church for the first time formulated a basic principle concerning the content and the very character of sacred art. It did so in response to a practical need. The canons of this council are not "a concession of the Church to the demands of the faithful," as modern scholarship maintains. The council was not limited to one particular subject, and not without reason.[1] As we shall see, what was given conciliar expression was the attitude of the Fathers toward sacred art, which constitutes the very tradition of the Church.

The Quinisext Council opened on September 1, 692. It is called "Quinisext" because it completes the two ecumenical councils which preceded it, the fifth in the year 554 and the sixth in the year 681, both held in Constantinople. Like the Sixth Ecumenical Council, the Quinisext was held in a "chamber" (*in Trullo*) of the imperial palace, whence the name sometimes given to it: "Synod in Trullo." The Fifth Council, which condemned Monophysitism, and the Sixth, which pro-

1 See A. Grabar, *L'Iconoclasme byzantin* (Paris, 1957), 79.

scribed Monotheletism, were concerned only with dogmatic questions. A whole series of disciplinary questions was waiting for a solution; it was to this end that the council was called. The Orthodox Church, therefore, considers it to be complementary to the two preceding councils, and it is even frequently referred to as the Sixth Ecumenical Council. The questions examined by the council concerned various aspects of ecclesiastical life. These included sacred art. "Some remains of the pagan and Jewish hesitancy have become mixed with the wheat ripe with truth." These words from a letter written by the Fathers of the council to Emperor Justinian II directly concern our subject, as we shall see.

Three canons of the Quinisext Council are concerned with sacred art. Canon 73 mentions the image of the cross:

> Given that the vivifying cross brought us salvation, we must strive in every possible way to show it the honor it deserves, since it saved us from the ancient fall. This is why, venerating it in thought, word and feeling, we order that all those images of the cross made on the ground by certain individuals be destroyed, so that this sign of our victory may not be trampled upon by the feet of those who walk. We order that those who trace the representation of the cross on the ground be henceforth excluded from communion.[2]

This is a simple order which needs no explanations: It is wrong to trace the image of the holy cross on the ground, since it risks being trampled on by the feet of passers-by.

Canon 82 is for us the most interesting. It is of critical importance because it shows us the content of the sacred image as the Church understands it. This canon specifies how this image developed. Following is the text:

> In certain reproductions of venerable images (γραφαῖς), the Forerunner is pictured pointing to the Lamb with his finger. This representation was adopted as a symbol of grace. It was a hidden figure of that true Lamb who is Christ our God, shown to us according to the Law. Having thus welcomed these ancient figures (τύπους) and shadows as symbols of the truth transmitted to the Church, today we prefer (προτιμῶμεν) grace and truth themselves, as a fulfillment of the Law. Therefore, in order to expose to the sight of all, at least with the help of painting, that which is perfect, we decree that henceforth Christ our God be represented in His human form (ἀνθρώπινον χαρακτῆρα) and not in the ancient form of the lamb. We understand this to be the elevation of the humility of God the Word, and we are led to remembering His life in the flesh, His

2   Rhalles and Potles, *Syntagma*, vol. 2 (Athens, 1852), 474.

passion, His saving death and, thus, deliverance (ἀπολυτρώσεως) which took place for the world.[3]

The first sentence of the canon explains the situation existing at that time. It speaks of St John the Baptist's (the "Forerunner") pointing out Christ, who is represented as a lamb. We know that the realistic image of Christ, His true portrait, existed from the beginning, and it is this portrait which is the true witness of His Incarnation. In addition, there were also larger cycles representing subjects from the Old and New Testaments, particularly those of our major feasts, where Christ was represented in His human form. And yet symbolic representations *replacing* the human image of Christ still existed in the seventh century. This belated attachment to biblical prefigurations, in particular to the image of the lamb, was particularly widespread in the West.[4] It was necessary, however, to guide the faithful toward the position adopted by the Church, and this is the purpose of Canon 82 of the Quinisext Council.

As we know, the lamb is an Old Testament symbol which played a very important role in the art of the first Christians. In the Old Testament, the paschal sacrifice of the lamb was the center of worship, just as the eucharistic sacrifice in the New Testament is the heart of the life of the Church, and Easter—the Feast of the Resurrection—is the center of the liturgical year. The unblemished lamb of Israel is the preeminent prefiguration of Christ. In the first centuries, when the direct image of the Savior was frequently hidden out of necessity, the image of the lamb was very widespread. Like the fish, it signified not only Christ, but also the Christian who imitated and followed Him.

The image of which the Quinisext Council speaks—Christ in the form of a lamb pointed out by St John the Baptist—was a very important dogmatic and liturgical image. It is based on a well-known passage of St John's Gospel (ch 1). The Gospel writer conveys the witness of St John the Baptist regarding the imminent coming of the Savior. The high priests and Levites had come to ask him whether he was Elijah or a prophet. But St John the Baptist, who was precisely the last of the Old Testament prophets, replies that he is the Forerunner of Him who comes directly

3   Rhalles and Potles, *ibid.*, 492.
4   "We do not know of a single representation of Byzantine origin where a lamb is pointed out by the Forerunner," writes N. Porkovsky, *Monuments of Christian Iconography and Art* (in Russian) (St Petersburg, 1900), 29.

after him. And, indeed, the very next day Christ appears before the people, asking St John to baptize Him, and the Forerunner points Him out saying: "Behold, the Lamb of God who takes away the sin of the world!" (Jn 1:29). The image which represents St John the Baptist designating the Lamb in this manner literally translates these words and fixes them in our memory. In forbidding this symbol, Canon 82 is inspired by the very same passage of the Gospel of St John. It interprets this text, however, not in isolation or literally, but in the context which precedes it, emphasizing not the *words* of St John the Baptist but *Him at whom John was pointing*. Indeed, the description of the appearance of Christ is preceded in the Gospel according to St John by a prologue which prepares for the manifestation of the Lord:

> And the Word became flesh and dwelt among us, full of grace and truth; we have beheld his glory, glory as of the only Son from the Father...And from His fullness have we all received grace upon grace. For the law was given through Moses; grace and truth came through Jesus Christ. *(1:14, 16–17)*

Because it is the *truth* which came through Jesus Christ, it is no longer a matter of translating a word into images, but of showing the truth itself, the fulfillment of the words. Indeed, when he was speaking of "the Lamb who takes away the sin of the world," it was not a lamb at which St John the Baptist was pointing but rather Jesus Christ Himself, the Son of God, who became Man and came to the world to fulfill the law and to offer Himself in sacrifice. It is He who was prefigured by the lamb of the Old Testament. It is this fulfillment, this reality, this truth which had to be shown to everyone. Thus, the truth had to be revealed not only in word but also in image: it had to be *shown*. Therein lies the most radical refusal of all abstractions, of every metaphysical view of religion. The truth has its own image, for it is not an idea or an abstract formula; it is a person, *The Person* "crucified under Pontius Pilate." When Pilate asks Christ, "What is truth?" (Jn 18:38), Christ only answers by remaining silent before him. Pilate leaves, without even awaiting an answer, knowing that a whole multitude of answers can be given to this question without one of them being valid. For it is the Church alone which possesses the answer to Pilate's question. Christ says to His apostles: "I am the way, and the truth, and the life" (Jn 14:6). The correct question is not "*What* is truth?" but rather "*Who* is the truth?" Truth is a person, and it has an image. This is why the Church not only *speaks* of the truth, but also *shows* the truth: the image of Jesus Christ.

The Fathers of the council continue: "Having thus welcomed these ancient figures and shadows as symbols of the truth transmitted to the Church, today we prefer grace and truth themselves, as a fulfillment of the law." Thus the Quinisext Council speaks of symbolic figures as of a stage already transcended in the life of the Church. If, at the beginning, the reference was to one symbolic figure only, the lamb, here, by contrast, the council mentions "figures and shadows" in general, undoubtedly seeing in the lamb not just one symbol among others, but the main symbol, the unveiling of which must naturally convey the unveiling of all the other symbolic figures.

The council orders that the symbols from the Old Testament, used in the first centuries of Christianity, be replaced by direct representations of the truth they prefigured. It calls for the unveiling of their meaning. The image contained in the symbols of the Old Testament becomes reality in the Incarnation. Since the Word became flesh and lived among us, the image must show directly that which happened in time and became visible, representable and describable.

Thus the ancient symbols are suppressed because a direct image now exists, and these symbols are belated manifestations of "Jewish hesitancy" toward direct images. As long as the wheat was not ripe, their existence was justified, even indispensable, since they contributed to its maturation. But in "the wheat ripe with truth," their role was no longer constructive. They even became a negative force, because they reduced the principal import-ance and role of the direct image. As soon as a direct image is replaced by a symbol, it loses the absolute importance it embodies.

After having prescribed the use of the direct image, Canon 82 formu-lates the dogmatic basis for this usage, and this is precisely where the essential value of this canon lies. For the first time, a conciliar decision formulates the link between the icon and the dogma of the Incarnation, the "life of Christ in the flesh." This christological basis of the icon will later be greatly developed by the defenders of icons during the iconoclastic period.

But Canon 82 does not limit itself to suppressing symbols and formu-lating the dogmatic principle which is the basis of the direct image. It also indicates, though indirectly, what this image should be. This image portrays the face of the incarnate God, the historical person of Jesus

Christ, who lived in a precise time and place. But the direct image of our Lord cannot be only an ordinary representation which recalls only His life, His suffering and His death. The contents of a sacred image cannot be limited to this, because the person represented is distinct from other men. He is not simply a man: He is the God-Man. An ordinary image can remind us of His life but cannot show us His glory, "the glorification of God the Word," according to the Fathers of the council. As a result, the representation simply of a historical event is not sufficient for an image to be an "icon." Using all the means available to figurative art, the image must show that He who is represented is the "Lamb who takes away the sins of the world, Christ our God." If the historical traits of Jesus, His portrait, are a witness to His coming in the flesh, to the abasement and the humiliation of the divinity, then the way in which this "Son of man" is represented must also reflect the glory of God. In other words, the humility of God the Word must be represented in such a way that, when looking at the image, we contemplate also His divine glory, the human image of *God the Word,* and that, in this way, we come to understand the saving nature of His death and the "resulting deliverance of the world."

The last part of Canon 82 indicates wherein the symbolism of sacred art lies: it must not be in the iconographic subject, in *what* is represented, but in *how* it is represented, in the means of representation. Thus the teaching of the Church is expressed not only by the *subject* of the image, but also by the *manner* in which such a subject is treated. In the realm of figurative art, the Church developed an artistic language that corresponded to its experience and to its knowledge of the divine revelation. It thereby puts us in direct contact with this revelation. All of the figurative possibilities of art converge toward the same goal: to convey faithfully a concrete, true image, a historical reality, and to reveal through it another reality, which is spiritual and eschatological.

Thus, on the one hand, the Quinisext Council required a direct image and discarded the symbols which did not represent Christ in His concrete humanity. It is impossible to refute a christological heresy with the image of a fish or of a lamb. Several years later, St Germanus, Patriarch of Constantinople, wrote to the iconoclast bishop Thomas: "The representation on icons of the image of the Lord in His human appearance confounds the heretics who claim that He became man only fictitiously, and not in reality."[5]

On the other hand, Canon 82 expresses for the first time the teaching of the Church on the icon, and simultaneously points out the possibility of conveying by artistic means a reflection of the divine glory, with the help of a certain symbolism. It emphasizes the great importance and ramifications of historical reality by recognizing that only the realistic image—represented in a certain way, by means of a symbolic language revealing a spiritual reality—is able to transmit Orthodox teaching. It holds that symbols, "figures and shadows," cannot express the fullness of grace, although they are worthy of respect, having corresponded to the needs of a given epoch. The iconographic symbol is, for all that, not completely excluded. But its importance is seen as secondary. Our own contemporary iconography still retains several of these symbols—for example, the three stars on the robe of the Virgin, which denote her virginity before, during and after the nativity, or else a hand descending from the sky to designate the divine presence. But this iconographic symbolism is relegated to a secondary place and never replaces the direct image.

Canon 82 expresses, for the first time, what we call the "iconographic canon," i.e., a set criterion for the liturgical quality of an image, just as the "canon of Scripture" establishes the liturgical quality of a text. The iconographic canon is a principle allowing us to judge whether or not an image is an icon. It establishes the conformity of the icon to Holy Scripture and defines in what this conformity consists: the authenticity of the transmission of the divine revelation in historical reality, by means of what we call symbolic realism, and in a way that truly reflects the Kingdom of God.

While Canon 82 was directed primarily against "Jewish hesitancy" by abolishing the Old Testament "figures and shadows," Canon 100 of the Quinisext Council is directed against "pagan immaturity." Its text reads as follows:

> Let your eyes look directly forward; keep your heart with all vigilance! [Prov 4:23, 25]. Wisdom demands it, for the bodily sensations easily enter the soul. We therefore ordain that misleading paintings which corrupt the intelligence (νοῦν) by arousing shameful pleasures, whether these are paintings (πίνακες)

5 *Epistolae*, PG 98: 173B.

or any other similar objects, not be fashioned in any way, and that anyone who undertakes to make such an object be excommunicated (ἀφοριζέσθω).[6]

It is hard to imagine that representations "arousing shameful pleasures" might have been used in the churches. But at the time of the Quinisext Council, in addition to the liturgical feasts, there still existed pagan feasts which the council prohibited in Canon 62—in particular the Bromalia, revels honoring Dionysus (Bacchus), dances honoring the ancient gods, and so forth. Such pagan feasts were naturally reflected in art, sometimes in the coarse form of shameless images. It is natural that the Church deemed it necessary to protect its members from the corrupting influence of such representations, all the more since certain elements from this art had infiltrated sacred art and had clouded its content. Canon 100 shows that the Church required that its members retain a certain asceticism not only in life, but also in an art which, on the one hand, reflects this life and, on the other, influences it. This concern for the moral aspect of art shows how seriously the Church took its mission. This canon reflects the fundamental principle that shows through clearly in all the patristic writings and in all sacred art, as we shall see.

The Quinisext Council marks the end of the dogmatic struggle of the Church in defense of the Orthodox confession of the two natures in Christ, His humanity and His Divinity. This is the moment when, according to the expression of the council Fathers, "piety is already proclaimed by us distinctly." These are the opening words of Canon 1 of the council. The Fathers and the councils had found clear and precise dogmatic formulations to express the teaching of the Church on the Incarnation of God, as much as it is possible to do this in words. The truth was proclaimed loudly and clearly. But this was not enough. The truth still had to be defended against those who did not accept it, despite the great clarity of the conciliar and patristic formulations. It was necessary not only to *speak* the truth, but also to *show* it. In the realm of the image, it was also necessary to make a rigorous confession which would stand up against the obscure and confused doctrines which everyone could accept equivocally, but which were not true. It was not a matter of finding a compromise to satisfy everyone, but of clearly confessing the truth, so "that this fulfillment might be seen by all," according to the words of Canon 82.

6   Rhalles and Potles, *Syntagma*, 545.

Through Canon 82, the Church responded to the attacks of the Jews of that time upon the Christian image; and through Canon 100 it discarded every vestige of Hellenistic art. Its answer to the needs of the moment carried a positive instruction: that the image can show "the glory of the Divinity becoming also that of the body," as St John of Damascus would say somewhat later.[7] For it is obvious that, at a time when christology was the main concern, it was precisely the human image of Christ, the basis of all Christian iconography, which demanded a dogmatic formulation against "the Jewish and pagan hesitancy."

The decisions of the Quinisext Council were signed by the emperor, and a place was left for the signature of the Pope of Rome; then appear the signatures of Patriarchs Paul of Constantinople, Peter of Alexandria, Anastasius of Jerusalem and George of Antioch. These were followed by the signatures of 213 bishops or their representatives. Among the signatures was that of Basil, Archbishop of Gortyna (in Crete), who had been entrusted by the Church of Rome to put its signature on the decisions of the council, and also those of the other western bishops.[8]

As soon as the council ended, the acts were sent to Rome requesting Pope Sergius' signature. He refused, even rejecting his copy of the acts. He declared that the decisions of the council had no value and asserted that he preferred death to accepting error. The "error" consisted undoubtedly in some teachings and practices concerning which there was a disagreement between the eastern churches and Rome, such as the mandatory celibacy of the clergy, the Saturday fast (already forbidden by the First Ecumenical Council), the representation of Christ in the form of a lamb, and others. Yet the Roman church eventually accepted the Seventh Ecumenical Council, which refers to Canon 82 of the Quinisext Council. Therefore, it can be said that the Roman Church implicitly also recognizes this canon. Pope St Gregory II refers to Canon 82 in his letter to the Patriarch of Constantinople, St Germanus.[9] Pope Hadrian I, for example,

---

7   *Homilia in transfigurationem Domini,* par. 23, PG 96: 564B.

8   Their power has been contested, even denied, by western scholars. Thus, in Héfélé-Leclercq, *Histoire des Conciles,* vol. 3 (Paris, 1909), 577, we read: "It is true that the *Vita Sergii* in the *Liber Pontificalis* reports that the legates of Pope Sergius, having been deceived by the emperor, signed their names. But these legates of the pope were simply pontifical apocrisiaries living in Constantinople and not legates who had been sent expressly to take part in the council."

9   Cited by G. Ostrogorsky, *Seminarium Kondakovianum,* 1 (Prague, 1927), 43.

solemnly declares his adherence to the Quinisext Council in his letter to
Patriarch St Tarasius; he does the same in a letter to the Frankish bishops
in defense of the Seventh Ecumenical Council. Pope John VIII spoke of
the decisions of the Quinisext Council without voicing any objection.
Later, Pope Innocent III, quoting Canon 82, calls the Quinisext Council
the Sixth Ecumenical Council. But all this is only the agreement of some
popes, whereas there were others who were of the opposite opinion. In
any case, the West never formannly accepted the decisions of the
Quinisext Council.

Thus, the teaching of the Church about the christological basis of the
icon has remained foreign to the Church of Rome. This teaching was
unable to enrich western sacred art, which even today remains attached to
certain purely symbolic representations, such as the lamb. The Church of
Rome excluded itself from the process of developing an artistic and
spiritual language, a process in which all the rest of the Church took an
active part, with the Church of Constantinople providentially becoming
the leader. The West remained outside of this development.

On the contrary, the Orthodox Church, in accordance with the
Quinisext Council, continued to refine its art in form and in content, an art
which conveys, through images and material forms, the revelation of the
divine reality, giving us a key to approach, contemplate and understand it.

It seems to us that it is particularly necessary for present-day Orthodoxy in the West to be well aware of the importance of Canon 82 of the
Quinisext Council. Indeed, this canon establishes a theoretical foundation for liturgical art. Whatever direction Orthodox art in the West might
take in the future, it will not be able to bypass the fundamental instruction which was first formulated in this canon: the transmittal of the
historical reality and of the revealed truth, expressed in certain forms that
correspond to the spiritual experience of the Church.

7

The Pre-Iconoclastic Period

The ancient world entered the Church slowly and with great difficulty. With its very sophisticated culture, it was like the rich man of whom Christ speaks: It would be more difficult for him to enter the Kingdom of God than for a camel to pass through the eye of a needle. The Church constantly borrowed from the heritage of antiquity in order to sacralize those elements which could be used to express the Christian revelation. It is natural that in this elaborate process of adaptation, certain elements of ancient art penetrated into the Church, elements which did not actually correspond to the meaning of sacred art, or even contradicted it. Their influence persisted, leaving behind carnal and sensual traits which remained in some monuments of sacred art, together with the illusory naturalism of antiquity, characteristic of paganism but foreign to the Christian faith. The Church never ceased to fight against these remnants of pagan art, and this struggle in the realm of art was simply the reflection of the struggle of the Church for its truth. In the realm of theology, heresy is the result of the human inability to accept divine revelation in its fullness, of the natural tendency to try to make this revelation more accessible, to lower the heavens down to earth. The same is true in the realm of sacred art. Secular art brought elements into the Church which "lowered" the revelation, which tried to make it more "accessible," more familiar, and thus corrupted the teaching of the Gospel, diverting it from its aim. As we shall see later, these same carnal and "illusory" elements, from the Italian Renaissance until today, will penetrate sacred art in the form of naturalism, idealism, etc. They will blur its purity and overwhelm it with elements of secular art.

In other words, the Church brings the image of Christ to the world, the image of man and of the world revived through the Incarnation, the saving image. The world, in turn, tries to introduce its own image into the

Church, the image of the fallen world, the image of sin, corruption and death. The words of the late Patriarch Sergius of Moscow are applicable here: "The world, hostile to Christ, will not only try to extinguish the light of Christ with persecutions and other external methods. The world will be able to penetrate into the very Manger of Christ."[1] In other words, it will try to destroy the Church from within. One of the ways that the world penetrates the Church is precisely through art. In this realm, the prince of this world always begins in the same way. He suggests to the faithful that art is art and nothing else, that it carries its own worth and that it can, in its own way, express the sacred in a secular and more accessible fashion, that it does not require a spiritual effort. And it is obviously much simpler to represent God in an image resembling fallen man than to try to do the opposite—to convey in the representation the image of God and the divine resemblance of man.

In Byzantium, the influence which the art of antiquity had on the Christian image was so important that it has led some scholars to speak of a "renaissance" of antiquity. Moreover, in the period that we are studying, the attitude of the faithful themselves towards the image, an attitude which frequently lacked true understanding, was a powerful weapon in the hands of those who were opposed to the veneration of images. Furthermore, attacks were made against the image from outside the Church, and this contributed to the development and consolidation of iconoclastic trends within the Church.

The christological controversies ended in the seventh century. During the first seven centuries of its life, the Church had defended its essential truth, which is the basis of our salvation: the truth of the divine Incarnation. It defended it point by point, formulating the various aspects of its teaching on the person of Jesus Christ, God and Man, giving the world the most exact definitions possible, which cut short all false interpretations. But once the partial attacks related to different aspects of christological doctrine were over, once the Church had triumphed over each heresy separately, a general offensive against the Orthodox teaching as a whole took place. Studying Canon 82 of the Quinisext Council, we saw its doctrinal significance and its historical necessity, for it presupposed that the image was a means of confessing Orthodoxy, just as it had been

1   *Patriarch Sergius and his Spiritual Heritage* (in Russian) (Moscow, 1947), 65.

confessed doctrinally during the preceding centuries. An open struggle against the icon came immediately afterwards, that is, a struggle against the confession of the Orthodox teaching of the image. One of the most terrible of heresies, undermining the very basis of Christianity, appeared—the iconoclasm of the eighth and ninth centuries.

There were many reasons for the spread of iconoclasm, which included, first of all, the misunderstandings, incomprehensions and abuses which distorted the veneration of icons. Some Christians zealously decorated churches and considered this to be sufficient for their salvation. St Amphilochius of Iconium denounced them already in the fourth century. Furthermore, there were ways of venerating sacred images which could be mistaken for blasphemy. Asterius of Amasea recounts in the seventh century that embroidered images of saints decorated the ceremonial robes of members of the Byzantine aristocracy.[2] In Alexandria, men and women walked on the streets dressed in clothing decorated with sacred images. An excessive veneration of icons was apparent in the practice admitted by the Church. Thus, icons sometimes served as godfathers or godmothers in baptism and at monastic tonsure. There were even stranger cases. Some priests scraped the colors off icons, mixed them with the Holy Gifts and distributed this mixture to the faithful as if the divine Body and Blood still had to be perfected with something sacred. Other priests celebrated the liturgy on an icon instead of an altar. The faithful, in turn, sometimes understood the veneration of icons too literally. They would venerate not so much the person represented on the image as the image itself. This practice clearly began to resemble magic or the decadent forms of paganism. All these facts created a great scandal for many believers who were not firm in Orthodoxy, and caused some of them to reject icons altogether.

But besides these erroneous attitudes towards icons, the images themselves were sometimes cause for scandal. The historical truth was often falsified. For example, St Augustine[3] informs us that during his time some artists arbitrarily represented Christ according to their own imagination, just as it often happens today. Some images scandalized the faithful by their subtle sensuality, which did not conform to the holiness of the

2   M. A. Vassiliev, *History of the Byzantine Empire*, vol. 1 (Madison, 1964), 256.
3   *De Trinitate*, VIII, ch. 14, par. 7, PL 42: 951-952.

person represented. Such images made the holiness of the icon—and indeed its very necessity for the Church—doubtful. Even worse, they provided the iconoclasts with a powerful weapon against sacred art in general. In their eyes, sacred art was not capable of reflecting the glory of God, the saints and the spiritual world. Its presence in the churches was a concession to paganism, as some of our contemporaries also believe. "How could one dare," they said, "represent by means of a vile Greek art the most glorious Mother of God, who received in her bosom the fullness of divinity, she who is higher than the heavens and more glorious than the cherubim?" Or else: "How can it not be shameful to represent, with the help of a pagan art, those who reign with Christ, who share His throne, judge the universe and resemble the image of His glory, when Scripture tells us that the whole world was not worthy of them?"[4]

Iconoclastic trends within the Church were strongly supported from outside the Church. We see in the acts of the Seventh Ecumenical Council that Anastasius the Sinaite had to defend icons, in the sixth century, against enemies unknown to us who had attacked them. Similarly, in the sixth century, St Simeon the Stylite, in his epistle to Emperor Justin II, speaks of Samaritans who insulted the icons of Christ and the Virgin. In the seventh century, Leontius, Bishop of Neapolis (Cyprus), wrote a work against iconoclasts who accused the Orthodox of idolatry on the basis of the Old Testament prohibition.[5] This same accusation was again refuted in the seventh century by John, Bishop of Thessalonica. Again in the eighth century, Bishop Stephen of Bostra in Arabia, a Moslem land, refuted the arguments of the Jews against icons in his work against the Jews.[6]

Among these different iconoclastic manifestations, it is the intervention of Islam which played the most important role. In the seventh century, the Moslem Arabs conquered Syria and Palestine and, after crossing Asia Minor, besieged Constantinople in 717. Emperor Leo III the Isaurian drove them back in 718. In the beginning of their rule over the territories they occupied, the Arabs were in general fairly tolerant toward Christian images. But the Jews, at the moment of the birth of

4   Acts of the Seventh Ecumenical Council, Sixth Session, Mansi XIII, 276, 277D.
5   PG 93: 597-1609, and Mansi XIII, 45.
6   See John of Damascus, *De imaginibus Oratio III*, PG 94(1): 1376BD.

Islam, again began to believe very firmly in the prohibition of the image by the Law of the Old Testament; they not only ceased decorating their synagogues with images, as they had done during the first centuries of Christianity, but, on the contrary, they destroyed the images which were found in them. The synagogues of Ain-Douq and Beth Alfa still show marks of this destruction.

In 723, Khalif Yezid abruptly gave an order to remove icons from all Christian churches in his territory. The Moslems, therefore, sought out icons, though it must be said that their persecutions were probably neither consistent nor systematic.

Besides Islam and Judaism, the iconoclastic camp also contained various Christian sects of a docetic tendency,[7] that is accepting the teaching that the Incarnation was illusory and unreal. These included, for example, the Paulicians and certain Monophysite groups.[8] At the Seventh Ecumenical Council, the Patriarch of Constantinople, St Tarasius, says that the iconoclasts were inspired by Jews, Saracens, Samaritans, Manichaeans and two Monophysite sects, the Phantasiasts and the Theopaschites.[9]

However one must not think that iconoclasm was only an Eastern heresy. It also appeared only in the West. But the West occupied only a "provincial" position in the Church in this period, and it was in the Eastern part of the Empire that the destiny of the Church was decided. It is therefore in the East that the heresy was the most violent and that the answer of the Church was also the most elaborate and effective. Iconoclasm did not become a systematic and organized heresy in the West, and

7 The best contemporary studies on iconoclasm are: M. G. Ostrogorsky, *Studien zur Geschichte des byzantinischen Bilderstreites* (Breslau, 1929); ch. 3 of his *Histoire de l'Empire byzantin*; and A. Grabar, *L'iconoclasme byzantin* (Paris, 1957).

8 The large majority of the Monophysites were not hostile to icons, and continue to have them even today. The Arians venerated neither saints, nor relics, nor icons. The great majority of the Nestorians venerated icons. The advocates of this heresy which exists even today (in the fourteenth century, as a result of the wars of Tamerlane, it experienced a great decline from which it never recovered) lost the veneration of icons but continue to venerate the cross. The Paulicians were a Manichaean dualistic sect. For them, matter had been created by an inferior and evil god, and was therefore contemptible. Christ had not assumed a real, material body, which is why He is absolutely unrepresentable. In the tenth century, Emperor John Tzimisces deported them to the European confines of the empire. Their dualistic and fanatically iconoclast doctrine spread in southern Europe. This led to a mass movement called, depending on the country, the movement of the Bogomils, of the Patarini, of the Cathars or Albigensians.

9 Fifth Session, Mansi XIII, 157D.

it appeared only in isolated cases both before and after Byzantine iconoclasm. One of the most characteristic episodes occurred at the end of the
sixth century. In 598 or 599, the Bishop of Marseille, Serenus, threw all
the icons out of the churches and had them destroyed under the pretext
that they were improperly worshipped by the people. Pope St Gregory the
Great praised the zeal with which the bishop opposed the worship of
images but criticized him for destroying them. "It was unnecessary," he
wrote, "to destroy the icons. They are exposed in the churches so that the
illiterate, looking at the walls, can read what they cannot read in books.
Brother, you should have preserved the icons, but not allowed the people
to worship them."[10] Having received the papal letter, Serenus tried to
question its authenticity. Therefore, in the year 600, St Gregory the Great
wrote to him again, demanding that he put an end to the trouble which
his act had provoked and that he place the icons back into the churches
and explain to the people how they should be venerated. St Gregory adds:

> We greatly praise the fact that you prohibited the worship of icons, but we forbid
> you to destroy them. It is necessary to distinguish between the worship of an
> icon and the process of learning through the icon that which must be worshipped
> in history. What the Scripture is for the man who knows how to read, the icon
> is for the illiterate. Through it, even uneducated men can see what they must
> follow. It is the book of those who do not know the alphabet. It follows that it
> is used instead of reading, especially for foreigners.[11]

But such iconoclastic manifestations in the West were only isolated cases;
they did not have the deep roots of Eastern iconoclasm, and therefore
could not have similar consequences.

---

10 *Epistolarum Liber IX, epist.* cv, PL 77: 1027C-1028A.
11 *Epostolarum Liber XI, epist.* xiii, PL 77: 1128A-1130A.

8

The Iconoclastic Period: A Synopsis

In the West, Interest In Byzantine Iconoclasm began at the time of the Reformation in the sixteenth-seventeenth centuries, when a bitter struggle took place concerning images. Since that time, numerous works have been devoted to iconoclasm, which is studied from the most varied perspectives.[1] Some scholars consider both religious and political factors, while others see the religious aspects as a mere pretext and seriously consider only political, social, and economic factors.

> For the modern researchers, the problems proper to iconoclasm... have turned out to be most obscure; the very fact that cultic religious questions were the object of a life and death struggle during an entire century seemed so incomprehensible that, contrary to all evidence from the sources, iconoclasm has been explained as a social reform movement. Where the data contradicted this interpretation, they were dismissed with supreme disdain; where documents were lacking for this scheme, they were invented.[2]

In other words, all such theories are only so many learned hypotheses, conditioned partially by doctrinal or ideological presuppositions,[3] or by

1 See M. Suzumov, "The Historiography of Iconoclasm" (in Russian), *Vizantiiskii Vremennik* XXII (1963), 199-226.

2 G. Ostrogorsky, "Über die vermeintliche Reformätigkeit der Isaurer," *Byzantinische Zeitschrift* 30 (1929-1930), 394-5. According to certain historians, Leo III decided to abolish icon-veneration to remove one of the chief obstacles to a closer relationship between Christians, Jews, and Moslems, and to facilitate their subjugation to the empire; it is also said that he wanted to free the people from the influence of the Church, and hence attacked the icons, its main instrument. Others maintain that "it was the intention of the iconoclastic emperors to take public education out of the hands of the clergy" (A. A. Vasiliev, *History of the Byzantine Empire*, vol. 1 [Madison, 1964], 252), or that the large number of monasteries was detrimental to the state. The many men who became monks reduced the number of agricultural workers, of soldiers for the army, and of civil servants (Ch. Diehl, *History of the Byzantine Empire* [New York, 1969], 58). We may recall that the estimated number of monks in the Byzantine empire at that time was about 100,000. By way of comparison, let us note that in Russia, at the beginning of this century, there were only 40,000 monks and nuns for a much larger population (A. A. Vasiliev, *op. cit.*, 256-7).

3 What is typical, in this sense, is the presentation of iconoclasm as being preeminently a struggle against monasticism. As strange as it may seem, such statements are made even today.

the personal sympathy of the authors for one or the other of the warring parties. In Byzantium, certainly, the doctrinal movements were linked in one way or another to political and social questions, and these played a more or less important role in the conflict.[4] Some of these questions could be closely linked to iconoclasm, others could coincide with it chronologically; still others could have influenced it to some degree, directly or indirectly. But all this was not the root of the problem. When, in evaluating the iconoclastic period, we leave the realm of speculation and turn to the documents and the facts, we see that they have an exclusively doctrinal character. These are the apologetic writings of the two factions, the acts of the councils and their decisions.

Iconoclasm existed before the state openly took a position in its favor; it continued to exist when this power not only renounced this ecclesiastic reform but took a hostile attitude toward it. Moreover, iconoclasm has repeated itself several times in the history of various countries, and with the same ideological presuppositions; it continues to exist in our day, without its being linked in the least to any political power.

In the Orthodox world, open iconoclasm began at the initiative of the state. In 726, Emperor Leo III the Isaurian, influenced by bishops from Asia Minor who were hostile to the worship of images and who had just been in Constantinople, openly took a position against the veneration of icons. Until today, scholarship has considered that he proclaimed two decrees to this effect: the first in 726, accepted unanimously by the Senate, the second in 730. The texts of both decrees are lost and certain modern scholars, for example G. Ostrogorsky,[5] assert that there was only

Thus, "one of the most important means in the struggle of the imperial government for absolute power was iconoclasm, directed against the monasteries" (G. Dombrovskii, *The Frescoes of Medieval Crimea* [in Russian] [Kiev, 1966], 14). However, we know from the documents that there were only a few personal attacks against monks who defended monasteries (see F. Dvornik, *The Photian Schism* [Cambridge, 1970], 69, note 1). Had monasteries been the main problem and the icon only a pretext, the weight of the polemic would have been on the issue of monasticism. However, we do not see anything like this in the writings of the iconoclastic period: not only the historic documents but also the specifically theological writings contain nothing either for or against monasticism as such. We do not see anything that could be compared to what is there about icons and their veneration.

4   G. Florovsky, *The Byzantine Fathers of the V-VIII Centuries* (in Russian) (Paris, 1933), and "Origen, Eusebius, and the Iconoclastic Controversy," *Church History* 19 (1950), 77. Thus, "even Monotheism itself was 'a political problem,' and 'the Caesaro-papalism' of the Iconoclast emperors was itself a kind of theological doctrine" (*ibid.*, 79).

5   "Les débuts de la querelle des images," *Mélanges Ch. Diehl,* vol. 1 (Paris, 1930), 235-55, and *Histoire de l'Etat byzantin,* 191-2.

one decree in 730, and that the years 726–730 were filled with futile attempts by the emperor to persuade Patriarch St Germanus (715–730) and Pope St Gregory II to adhere to iconoclasm. In any case, St Germanus categorically refused to sign the imperial decree. He announced to the emperor that he would not tolerate any change in the teaching of the faith without an ecumenical council. This is why St Germanus had to suffer humiliation and be deposed, deported and replaced by an iconoclast, Patriarch Anastasius (730–753). Thus, the iconoclastic decree which appeared in 730 was not only signed by the emperor, but also by the patriarch. In other words, it was proclaimed not only by the state, but also by the hierarchy of the Church of Constantinople. After the decree of 730, icons began to be destroyed everywhere.

The first iconoclastic act, by order of the emperor, was to destroy an icon of Christ above one of the entrances to the imperial palace. The destruction of this icon provoked a popular uprising; the civil servant sent by the emperor to smash it was killed and the murderer was harshly punished by the emperor. A fierce struggle began, marked by the blood of martyrs and confessors. Orthodox bishops were exiled, the faithful laity were persecuted by torture and death. This struggle lasted just over one hundred years and can be divided into two periods. The first stretches from 730 to 787, the date of the Seventh Ecumenical Council, which, under the rule of the Empress Irene, reestablished the worship of icons and formulated the dogma of their veneration. The second lasted from 814 to 843.

In reality, the attack against the veneration of icons represented an illegitimate intervention of civil power in the realm of the Church, in its liturgical life and in its teaching. Emperor Leo III was a despotic and brutal man. For example, he compelled Jews and Montanists to be baptized; they sometimes preferred suicide. For the iconoclasts, caesaropapism, the power of the state in Church affairs, was a normal principle. "I am an emperor and priest" (βασιλεὺς καὶ ἱερεὺς εἰμί), Leo II wrote to Pope Gregory II.[6] In response to this principle, St John of Damascus, in his second apology *On the Divine Images,* expressed the point of view of the Church:

> We will obey you, O emperor, in those matters which pertain to our daily lives: payments, taxes, tributes; these are your due and we will give them to you. But as far as the government of the Church is concerned, we have our pastors, and they have

6   Mansi XXI, 975.

preached the word to us; we have those who interpret the ordinances of the Church.[7]

The Orthodox position was very clear and uncompromising from the beginning. Thus, Patriarch St Germanus, who wrote three dogmatic epistles to the iconoclastic bishops even before the explicit manifestations of iconoclasm, preferred humiliation and exile to heresy. Immediately after the imperial decree, St John of Damascus responded with the first of his three treatises *In the Defense of Holy Icons*. This treatise, like the other two, not only represents a response to the iconoclastic theory, but also a very complete and systematic theological exposition of the Orthodox teaching on the image.

At the beginning of iconoclasm, the Pope of Rome was St Gregory II. Like Patriarch St Germanus, he refused to submit to the emperor, and, in 727, he called together a council which confirmed the veneration of icons, referring to the tabernacle of the Old Testament and to the image of the cherubim in it. Most of Italy revolted against the emperor, and the insurgents declared that they would place another emperor on the throne of Constantinople. St Gregory II wrote letters to the emperor and the patriarch which were later read at the Seventh Ecumenical Council. In 731 his successor, Gregory III, a Greek from Syria, called together a new council in Rome, where it was decided that:

> In the future, whoever removes, destroys, dishonors or insults the images of the Savior, His Holy Mother (*Virginis immaculatae atque gloriosae*), or the apostles...will not receive the Body and Blood of the Savior and will be excluded from the Church.[8]

Gregory III zealously decorated the churches and ordered icons to be painted. Honoring the insulted saints, he instituted in the chapel of St Peter in Rome the Feast of All Saints, until now only a local celebration.

The struggle for and against icons which raged in the East and in the West was primarily concentrated in the Church of Constantinople. The other patriarchs of the East were, at the time, under Moslem rule and did not suffer from the systematic persecution which raged in the Byzantine Empire.

The first period of iconoclasm reached its paroxysm during the reign of Constantine Copronymus, the son of Leo III (741–755).[9] He was an

---

7   *De imaginibus oratio II*, ch. 12, PG 94(1): 1297; *On the Divine Images*, trans. D. Anderson (New York: St Vladimir's Seminary Press, 1980), 60.

8   Héfélé, *Histoire des Conciles*, vol. 3 (Paris, 1910), part 2, 677.

9   At the beginning of his reign, there was a short interval of 16 months when the veneration of icons was restored by the usurper Artavasdus.

even more fanatical iconoclast than his father, and the three patriarchs who succeeded each other in the see of Constantinople during his reign were completely dependent on him. The first ten years of Constantine's reign were relatively quiet, for he was engaged in political struggles to maintain his rule. But then, persecution of the Orthodox broke loose with a violence which was comparable to that under Diocletian. Constantine wrote a treatise in which he summarized the iconoclastic doctrine, and he called together a council. Neither the treatise of the emperor nor the acts of the council were preserved, for they were later burned; but we know the contents of both. The treatise of Constantine is frequently quoted in a polemical work by Patriarch St Nicephorus, and the decisions of the iconoclastic council of 754 were recorded in the polemical section of the acts of the Seventh Ecumenical Council. The emperor's treatise is very violent in tone and expresses an extreme position, suppressing the cult of the Virgin and of the saints. Moreover, Constantine Copronymus later published a decree suppressing the name "Mother of God" and forbidding the use of the word "saint." Overly frequent visits to churches were forbidden, and so was celibacy. The emperor's treatise was written on the eve of the iconoclastic council, which had been cleverly prepared. Presided over by the Bishop of Ephesus, Theodosius,[10] it began on February 10, 754, in Hieria, and ended August 8 in the church of Blachernae in Constantinople. Three hundred thirty-eight bishops participated, an impressive number. These were the iconoclasts who had replaced the deposed Orthodox bishops. For some of them, new episcopal sees had been created by the emperor.[11] It was decided at the council that whoever painted or possessed icons would be deprived of his priesthood if he were a priest, and excommunicated if he were a monk or a layman. The guilty were delivered to a civil tribunal, and questions of faith were thus made subject to the jurisdiction of public power.[12] At the close of the council, the confessors of Orthodoxy, St Germanus, St John of Damascus and St

10 Patriarch Anastasius died in 753, and his successor, Constantine, was named by the emperor and presented to the council only at its last session. See G. Ostrogorsky, *History*, 201-2.

11 To understand the composition of the council to be an active minority (the iconoclasts) on the one hand, and a passive majority (the Orthodox) on the other, as is done by A. Schmemann (*The Historical Road of Eastern Orthodoxy*, [New York, 1963], 205), does not correspond to the historical situation. In fact, the venerators of icons were not represented at the council at all (Cf. G. Ostrogorsky, *History*, 200).

12 See A. A. Vasilev, *History*, vol. 1, 260.

George of Cyprus, were excommunicated.[13] The faithful were required to make an iconoclastic confession of faith, and the persecutions became particularly cruel.

In spite of all this, the faithful populace did not allow themselves to be fooled and did not renounce the veneration of icons. The leaders of Orthodoxy were the monks, those "idolaters and worshippers of the shadows," as Constantine Copronymus called them. They were fiercely persecuted. Their heads were shattered against icons, they were sewn into sacks and drowned, they were forced to break their monastic vows, and the hands of iconographers were burned. Monks emigrated in groups, particularly to Italy, Cyprus, Syria and Palestine.[14] According to some historians, Italy alone received 50,000 of these monks during the time of Leo III and Constantine Copronymus. Many of them were iconographers, which is why the city of Rome never produced more works of sacred art than during the iconoclastic epoch. All the popes who succeeded one another during the reign of Constantine Copronymus (Zacharias, Stephen II, Paul I, Stephen III and Hadrian I) remained firm in the Orthodox faith and continued the work of their predecessors in decorating churches with icons, with the help of monk-iconographers who had emigrated from the Eastern part of the Empire.[15]

With the death of Constantine Copronymus, the persecutions became less violent. His son, Leo IV, was a moderate and rather indifferent iconoclast. At his death in 780, his wife Irene came to the throne with her underage son, Constantine. Being an Orthodox who had never ceased venerating icons, Irene immediately began restoring Orthodoxy. The Orthodox candidate to the patriarchal throne was Tarasius (784-806). Under his influence, the empress began to prepare for the Seventh Ecumenical Council. However, as soon as this council began its work in Constantinople, the troops revolted, urged to do so by the iconoclastic bishops, and did not allow the council to continue. But soon after, when these troops were replaced by others, Irene resumed her attempt, and the council was convened in Nicaea in 787 (Fig.

13   Mansi XIII, 356C-D.
14   Andreev, *Germanus and Tarasius, Patriarchs of Constantinople* (in Russian) (Sergiev Posad, 1907), 70.
15   It is during this period that Santa Maria Antiqua was decorated in Rome. During the second iconoclastic period, the cathedral of St Mark was rebuilt and the churches of Santa Maria in Domnica, St Praxeda, and St Cecilia were built and decorated.

12. *The Seventh Ecumenical Council*

12). Three hundred fifty bishops and many monks participated. An imperial decree and an address of Patriarch Tarasius guaranteed freedom of speech, and the heretics were invited to put forth their doctrine. In response, on the Orthodox side, a deacon read refutations point by point. The council reestablished the veneration of icons and relics and took a series of steps to reestablish normal life in the Church.

However, the Orthodox teaching on the sacred image was not accepted by its adversaries. As has often happened in the history of the Church, both before and after iconoclasm, all did not want to accept the truth which had been solemnly proclaimed. Peace only lasted for twenty-seven years. Then the second iconoclastic period began.

Nicephorus I, a rather lukewarm Orthodox who did not take a stand either for or against icons, ruled after Empress Irene. But his successor, Leo V the Armenian (813-820), discovered that iconoclastic emperors had had better political and military luck than Orthodox emperors. This is why he decided to return to iconoclasm. He asked John the Grammarian, "the brain of the iconoclastic 'renaissance',"[16] to compose a treatise based on the decisions of the earlier iconoclastic council. Thus these decisions, which had already received a complete Orthodox answer, were artificially resurrected to serve the political aims of the emperor. The second wave of iconoclasm, like the first, was a violation of the sovereignty of the Church in its internal realm by the power of the state. But the emperor did not find the support in the episcopate which Constantine Copronymus had enjoyed. When, in 814, John the Grammarian had finished his work, the emperor began a discussion with Patriarch St Nicephorus I (810-815) in an attempt to reach a compromise which would forbid the veneration of icons without suppressing them completely. The emperor did not use threats; he earnestly asked, in the name of the peace of the Church, that concessions be made to iconoclasm. But the holy patriarch refused to make any compromises. St Theodore the Studite, who with 270 other monks took part in the discussion, told the emperor that he had no right to meddle in the internal life of the Church. The negotiations were never completed and persecutions began. The patriarch first saw his powers limited, and then, in 815, he was dismissed, exiled and replaced by an iconoclast, Theodotus I (815-821). The same

16   G. Ostrogorsky, *History*, 231.

year, a new iconoclastic council, presided over by Patriarch Theodotus, was called together in Constantinople, at the cathedral of Hagia Sophia. It was neither as significant nor as large as the first. In general, iconoclasm lost much of its doctrinal vitality during this second period. The iconoclasts could say nothing new and were therefore limited to continuously repeating the old arguments, already refuted by the Orthodox.[17] This time, the council emphasized that it did not consider icons to be idols,[18] but this in no way lessened their destruction; and even though there was nothing new or valid in the iconoclastic doctrine, the persecutions only became more violent, reaching the magnitude of those under Constantine Copronymus. Monks were again persecuted, and icons, books and sacred vases with images were destroyed. Iconoclasm was taught in schools and appeared in manuals.[19]

Another turnabout occurred when Emperor Michael II came to the throne in 821. Though an iconoclast, he recalled the Orthodox from exile and from prison. His reign was a calm one. But the situation changed again during the reign of Michael's son, Emperor Theophilus. When John the Grammarian came to the patriarchal throne in 837, a new wave of persecutions began.[20]

When Emperor Theophilus died in January, 842, his widow Theodora became the regent for his son Michael III, who was underage. She was Orthodox, and the worship of icons was decidedly reestablished by a council held in Constantinople in 843 under Patriarch St Methodius (842-846). The council confirmed the dogma of the veneration of icons which had been

17 The doctrine promulgated at this second iconoclastic council is known through a letter of Emperor Michael to Louis the Pious (Mansi 14: 417-422) and by the *Refutations* of St Theodore the Studite, but particularly by the response of Patriarch St Nicephorus, who quoted it freely.

18 G. Ostrogorsky, *Studien zur Geschichte des byzantinischen Bilderstreites* (Breslau, 1929), 51, and *History*, 232.

19 Thus the great defender of icons, St Theodore the Studite, was dragged from one prison to another and was beaten so unmercifully that his bruised flesh rotted alive; and his faithful disciple, St Nicholas the Studite, who never left him, was compelled to remove this rotten flesh with a knife.

20 It was at this time that the monk-iconographer, St Lazarus, suffered martyrdom. Having been cruelly beaten, with this hands burned, he dragged himself directly from the execution place to the church of St John the Baptist and started to paint his icon. The learned Theodore and Theophanes, who at the request of the Patriarch of Jerusalem raised their voices against iconoclasm, were cruelly beaten several times. Moreover, an insulting inscription was marked on their faces with a red hot iron. This is why the Church venerates them as Theodore and Theophanes the "marked" (*graptoi*).

established by the Seventh Ecumenical Council, excommunicated the iconoclasts and established, in March, 843, the feast of the Triumph of Orthodoxy on the first Sunday of Lent, with the exaltation of icons in all churches.

It is important to note that iconoclasm did not renounce art as such. Iconoclasts were not enemies of art. On the contrary, they promoted it. They persecuted only the representations of Christ, of the Virgin and of the saints. Thus the iconoclasm of the eighth and ninth centuries can be likened to Western Protestantism, with the difference that the iconoclasts did not leave the walls of the churches bare. On the contrary, they took great pleasure in decorating them with secular subjects, landscapes, representations of animals, etc. Purely decorative shapes also played a large role. Iconoclastic art was both a return to Hellenistic origins and a borrowing from the Moslem East. Emperor Theophilus, in particular, was a pompous prince and a great builder, who strongly encouraged monumental art. He had a palace built in the style of those of Baghdad, its walls covered with incrustations, mosaics and paintings of shields, weapons, all kinds of animals, trees, and flowers. He decorated churches in this same style.[21] When sacred images were removed everywhere, they were replaced with animals and birds. Constantine Copronymus had earlier served as a remarkable example: In the church of Blachernae, for example, he destroyed a series of biblical images and replaced them with "flowers, different birds and other animals, surrounded by plants, among which cranes, crows and peacocks stirred." The emperor was reproached for having transformed the church, with such images, into "an orchard and an aviary." [22] He also replaced a fresco representing the Sixth Ecumenical Council with a portrait of his favorite coachman.

In the West, during the second iconoclastic period, Pope Pascal I and Pope Gregory IV continued to defend and propagate sacred images. In 835, i.e., during the persecution of Theophilus, Pope Gregory IV decreed that the Feast of All Saints, which had been instituted by Gregory III, was to be celebrated by all of Christianity on November 1. In general in the West, both in Rome and in other areas, the iconoclastic persecutions encouraged the worship of saints and of their relics. It is during the iconoclastic period that the relics of many saints were brought to France

21   A. Grabar, *L'Iconoclasme byzantin* (Paris, 1957), 169-70, 171.
22   Ch. Diehl, *Manuel d'Art byzantin*, vol. 1 (Paris, 1925), 365-6.

(for example, those of St Guy in 751, of St Sebastian in 826 to the church of St Medard in Soissons, and of St Helen in 840 to Hautevilliers, near Reims).[23]

As we can see, the Church of Rome did not succumb to the temptation of iconoclasm. On the contrary, it remained firm in its belief in the veneration of icons, saints and their relics, in contrast to the iconoclasm of the Church of Byzantium.

---

23   Iconoclasm also had other consequences in the West. When the Lombards were threatening Rome, the Pope, rather than ask an iconoclastic emperor for help, turned to Pepin the Short, who, having saved Rome from the barbarians, in effect created the papal state in 756, thus making the Pope a temporal sovereign.

9

The Teaching of the Iconoclasts and the Orthodox Response

The scope of the iconoclastic ideology extends beyond the limits of the heresy fought during the eighth and ninth centuries. There is, in different forms, a permanency to iconoclasm. Suffice it to think of the Albigensians in medieval France, the Judaizers in fifteenth-century Russia, and finally, of the Protestant Reformation. This is why the theological answer of the Church to the iconoclastic heresy of the eighth and ninth centuries continues to be valid even today.

From the doctrinal point of view, the only one to be decisive, iconoclasm is a complex phenomenon which has not sufficiently been studied as a heresy. It has been observed many times[1] that Christology formed the common core of the questions that divided the two parties, the Orthodox and the heterodox, during the dogmatic struggle of the eighth and ninth centuries. However, iconoclasm has appeared in numerous forms.

At the beginning, the positions of the iconoclasts were very unsophisticated. To the Orthodox, they made more or less the same reproaches as certain Protestants make today: they accused them of idolizing stones, boards, and walls. Soon, two trends developed within iconoclasm.

Partisans of the first trend demanded the complete destruction of sacred images, starting with the icon of Christ. Some also rejected the veneration of relics, while the most intolerant of them went so far as to suppress the cult of the Virgin and of the saints. This trend is interesting because, in its very violence, it is the most consequential and logical, and clearly shows where the denial of icons, with the web of errors attached to it, is to lead.

Alongside this trend, there was another that was more tolerant, and which itself included many shadings. Its advocates allowed holy images in

---

1 To mention only one work among the most recent, Chr. von Schönborn, O.P., *L'icône du Christ. Fondements théologiques* (Freiburg, 1976).

the Church, but disagreed about the attitude to be taken towards them. Some said that the icon did not have to be venerated at all; others acknowledged the icon of Christ, but not those of the Virgin and of the saints; still others maintained that Christ Himself should be represented only before His resurrection, and that He was no longer representable afterwards.

From the very beginning of the catastrophe, the apologists of Orthodoxy took a very clear dogmatic position; they insisted on arguments of a christological nature to support the existence of icons. However, Ostrogorsky notes,

> a scholarly opinion became widespread, how this happened is not known, according to which proofs of a christological order were not used by the venerators of icons before the iconoclastic council of 754. Only this council's recourse to arguments of that type in favor of the iconoclastic thesis would have forced the Orthodox also to resort to them. If this were really the case, that is, if the christological arguments were really put forth by the Orthodox only in response to similar methods used by their adversaries, the whole issue would have been a dialectical, scholastic exercise at the most, and there would have been no question of the crucial importance of Christology in the struggle for the icon. But this was not the case. We maintain that the question of icons was, from the beginning, linked by the Orthodox to christological teaching, whereas their opponents gave them no pretext for this.[2]

After citing proofs taken from the surviving writings of Orthodox apologists of this period (Patriarch St Germanus, St John of Damascus, Pope St Gregory II, and St George of Cyprus), G. Ostrogorsky continues:

> Furthermore, there is no evidence from the historical documents that during the first period of the struggle the iconoclasts had accused the icon venerators of anything except idolatry. Thus, it would certainly be more legitimate to state that the christological arguments of the iconoclastic council were nothing but a forced reply to the arguments of the Orthodox party, rather than the opposite. Such an assertion would, in any case, not contradict the historical data as does the contrary assertion, which is so often expressed.[3]

The teaching of the Church and the christological basis of the icon had already been exposed by the Quinisext Council, even before the start of iconoclasm. It is also before its beginning, at the end of the seventh century, that Bishop John of Thessalonika appealed to the christological

---

2   G. Ostrogorsky, "The Works of the Orthodox Apologists" (in Russian), *Seminarium Kondakovianum* I (Prague, 1927), 36.

3   *Ibid.*, 44, note.

basis of the icon in his polemics against the pagans and the Jews. Similarly, in his three epistles to the iconoclastic bishops Thomas of Claudiopolis, John of Sinada and Constantine of Nacolea, St Germanus uses the Incarnation to justify the existence of icons.[4] These epistles were written before the open attack against the veneration of icons launched by Emperor Leo III. Canon 82 of the Quinisext Council is the basis for the Orthodox line of thinking, and the holy Patriarch Germanus repeats the christological section almost verbatim in his work *On Heresies and Councils.*[5]

From the beginning of iconoclasm, the Orthodox understood the danger it presented to the fundamental dogma of Christianity. Indeed, if the very existence of the icon is based on the Incarnation of the second person of the Holy Trinity, this Incarnation, in turn, is confirmed and proven by the image. In other words, the icon is a proof that the divine Incarnation was not an illusion. This is why, in the eyes of the Church, the attack against the icon of Christ is an attack on His Incarnation and on the whole economy of our salvation. This is why, in defending sacred images, the Church was not only defending their didactic role or their aesthetic aspect, but the very basis of the Christian faith. This explains the resolution of the Orthodox in defense of the icon, their intransigence, and their willingness to suffer greatly.

The iconoclastic argumentation—the accusation of idolatry and the appeal to the Old Testament—clashed with a well-articulated and clearly formulated theology, and turned out to be insufficient. Faced with the strong and unwavering position of the Orthodox, a theological basis for iconoclasm had to be found, and the heresy found its theoretician in the person of Emperor Constantine V Copronymus. Taking into account the Orthodox argumentation and responding to it, Constantine composed a treatise, the content of which reveals the deep split that separated Orthodoxy from iconoclasm. All the iconoclastic trends, pushed to the extreme, are gathered there. This work of the emperor, containing his point of view about the very concept of the icon, was presented to the iconoclastic council in 754. The council could not accept everything in this treatise and had to moderate some of its points. Thus it did not condemn the

4   *Epistolae,* PG 98: 164-193, 156-161, 161-164.
5   *De haeresibus et synodis,* PG 98: 80A.

veneration of the Virgin and of the saints; however, Constantine later succeeded in imposing these doctrines also. The imperial treatise also contained expressions so grossly monophysitic that the council felt obliged to modify them, and, in order to justify iconoclasm, it directed the accusation of monophysitism against the Orthodox, as we shall see. Neither the Patriarchs of the East nor the Pope of Rome were represented at the council. Its last meeting concluded with a solemn procession of all the participants in the public square, and with the reading of the iconoclastic profession of faith before the crowd, with the excommunication of the leading confessors of Orthodoxy. After a short introduction, this profession of faith begins by listing the six ecumenical councils and the heresies they condemned; then it states that the council of 754 is in line with the ecumenical councils and is perfectly orthodox. Next, the veneration of icons is declared to have its origin in idolatry inspired by the devil, and opposed by both the Old and New Testaments. The text then moves on to the argumentation; first, it enumerates the theological arguments, then the biblical and patristic ones.

We will deal briefly with the general aspects of this argumentation, and especially with the very concept of the icon as understood in iconoclastic thought. What was an icon for an iconoclast? What was its nature? What does it have in common with the person represented, and how is it differentiated from this person? Indeed, the essential difference between the two sides lay in the very definition of "icon": the term "icon" was understood differently by the iconoclasts and by the Orthodox.

The iconoclastic notion of the icon is clearly and precisely expressed in Emperor Constantine's treatise, which conveys the point of view shared by all the leaders of iconoclasm. According to him, a true icon must be of the same nature as the person it represents; it must be consubstantial with its model (ὁμοούσιον). Basing themselves on this principle, the iconoclasts came to the inevitable conclusion that the only icon of Christ is the Eucharist. Christ, they said, chose bread as the image of His Incarnation because bread has no human likeness, and thus idolatry can be avoided.

The very idea of an "image," of an "icon," meant something entirely different in iconoclastic thought than it did in Orthodox thought; because for the iconoclasts, only something identical to its prototype could be considered to be a real icon, only the Holy Gifts could be confessed as an icon of Christ. But for the Orthodox, the Holy Gifts are not an icon precisely because they are identical to their prototype.[6]

In fact, the "change" of the Holy Gifts does not make them into an image, but into "the most pure Body and the most precious Blood" of Christ. This is why the very act of calling the Eucharist an "image" was foreign and incomprehensible to the Orthodox. The Fathers of the Seventh Ecumenical Council responded to this reasoning by stating that "neither the Lord, nor the Apostles, nor the Fathers, ever used the term 'image' to speak of the unbloody sacrifice offered by the priest, but always called it the very Body and Blood."[7]

> For the Orthodox, not only was the icon not consubstantial with (ὁμοούσιον) or identical to (ταυτό) its prototype, as it was for the iconoclasts, but on the contrary, according to the Orthodox apologists, the very idea corresponding to the word 'icon' (εἰκών) implies an essential difference between the image and its prototype.[8]

> ...because the representation is something different from that which is represented.[9]

This is why the holy Patriarch Nicephorus finds this theory that the image has the same nature as its prototype "senseless and ridiculous."[10] He explains that

> the icon bears a resemblance to the prototype...or it is an imitation of the prototype and its reflection, but by its nature (τῇ οὐσίᾳ καὶ τῷ ὑποκειμένῳ), it is distinguishable from its prototype. An icon resembles its prototype because of the perfection of imitating art, but it is distinguishable from its prototype by its nature. And if it were not distinguishable from its prototype, it would not be an icon, but it would be the prototype itself.[11]

St Theodore the Studite expresses himself more bluntly: "No one could be so foolish as to think that reality and its shadow...the prototype and its representation, the cause and the consequence are by nature (κατ' οὐσίαν) identical."[12]

Patriarch Nicephorus certainly grasped the very essence of the question when,

6   G. Ostrogorsky, "The Foundations of the Controversy About the Holy Icons" (in Russian), *Seminarium Kondakovianum* II (Prague, 1928).
7   Sixth Session, Mansi XXXI, 274.
8   G. Ostrogorsky, *Seminarium Kondakovianum* II, 48.
9   St John of Damascus, *De imaginibus oratio III*, ch. 16, PG 94(1): 1337, *passim.*
10   *Antirrheticus.*, PG 100:225ff.
11   *Ibid.*, PG 100: 277A.
12   *Ibid.*, PG 99: 341B.

having indicated the difference between an image and its prototype, he asserts that those who do not accept this difference, who do not understand it, can rightly be called idolaters.[13]

In fact, if the icon were identified with the person it represents, it would be impossible for an even slightly developed religious conscience to venerate icons. Everyone agrees on this. And the person who was unable to understand a relationship other than that of essential identity obviously had to repudiate all veneration of icons. On the other hand, the question of idolatry could not even come up for the person who saw, in the very notion of the image, "the essential difference between the image and the person being represented and with whom the icon was only connected in a certain way."[14]

Thus, iconoclastic thought could accept an image only when this image was identical to that which it represented. Without identity, no image was possible. Therefore an image made by a painter could not be an icon of Christ. In general, figurative art was a rejection of the dogma of the divine Incarnation. "What then does the ignorant painter do when he gives a form to that which can only be believed in the heart and confessed with words?," asked the iconoclasts. "The name of Jesus Christ is the name of the God-Man. Therefore," they said, "you commit a double blasphemy when you represent Him. First of all, you attempt to represent the unrepresentable divinity. Second, if you try to represent the divine and human natures of Christ on the icon, you risk confusing them, which is monophysitism. You answer that you only represent the visible and tangible flesh of Christ. But this flesh is human and, therefore, you represent only the humanity of Christ, only His human nature. But, in this case, you separate it from the divinity which is united with it, and this is Nestorianism. In fact, the flesh of Jesus Christ is the flesh of God the Word; it had been completely assumed and deified by Him. How, then, do these godless persons," asserts the decision of the iconoclastic council, "dare to separate the divinity from the flesh of Christ and represent this flesh alone, as the flesh of an ordinary man? The Church believes in Christ who inseparably and purely united in Himself divinity and humanity. If you only represent the humanity of Christ, you separate His two natures, His divinity and His humanity, by giving this humanity its

13 *Ibid.*, PG 100: 277B.
14 G. Ostrogorsky, *Seminarium Kondakovianum* II, 50-1.

own existence, an independent life, seeing in it a separate person and thus introducing a fourth person into the Holy Trinity."[15] In other words, the iconoclasts believe that an icon cannot express the relationship which exists between the two natures of Christ. It is therefore impossible to make His icon, that is, to represent with human means the God-Man. This is why the Eucharist is the only possible icon of the Lord. G. Ostrogorsky writes that "it is characteristic that certain modern scholars, and particularly Protestant theologians, consider such reasoning not only to be well-founded, but also irrefutable, not seeing that it is simply missing the point."[16]

As can be seen, the iconoclasts, in their argumentation, wished to place themselves in the realm of the dogma of Chalcedon. But the flaw in their reasoning, which those who defended icons did not fail to point out, consisted precisely in their basic understanding of the dogma of the God-Man. Chalcedon makes a very clear distinction between *nature* on the one hand, and *person* or *hypostasis* on the other. It is precisely this clarity which is lacking in iconoclastic thought. The iconoclasts see only two possibilities in the image of the incarnate God the Word: Either, in representing Christ, we represent His divine nature, or, in representing the man Jesus, we represent His human nature distinct from His divinity. Both possibilities are heretical. There is no third option.

But the Orthodox, fully aware of the distinction between nature and person, maintain precisely this third possibility, which abolishes the iconoclastic dilemma. The icon does not represent the nature, but the person: Περιγραπτὸς ἄρα ὁ Χριστὸς καθ' ὑπόστασιν κἄν τῇ θεότητι ἀπερίγραπτος, "Christ is describable according to His hypostasis, remaining indescribable in His Divinity," explains St Theodore the Studite (Fig. 13).[17] When we represent our Lord, we do not represent His divinity or His humanity, but His Person, which inconceivably unites in itself these two natures without confusion and without division, as the Chalcedonian dogma defines it.

The Monothelites of old had attributed to the person that which was part of the nature. Christ is a person, they said, and therefore He has only

15 Abridged from the iconoclastic *horos.* See Héfélé, *Histoire des Conciles* (Paris, 1910), 697-703.
16 G. Ostrogorsky, *Seminarium Kondakovianum* II, 50, note 1.
17 *Antirrheticus IV*, ch. 34, PG 99: 405B.

13. *St Theodore the Studite*

one will, one action. In contrast, the iconoclasts attributed to the nature that which belongs to the person. From here stems the confusion in iconoclastic thought. If will and action are characteristic of both natures of Jesus Christ, so that He has two wills and two actions which correspond to His two natures, then His image is not characteristic of either of His natures, but of His person, of His hypostasis. The icon is not an image of the divine nature. It is an image of a divine person incarnate; it conveys the features of the Son of God who came in the flesh, who became visible and could therefore be represented with human means. The Orthodox did not even ask the question of nature. Aware of the primordial difference between nature and person, they clearly understood that an icon, like an ordinary portrait, could only be a personal image, because "nature does not exist alone, but appears in persons," as St John of Damascus explains.[18] In other words, nature exists only in persons, and each person fully possesses his own nature. Each Person of the Trinity possesses the fullness of the divine nature; each human being possesses the fullness of human nature. Nature is the same in all people, but there are many persons, and each of them is unique and irreplaceable. When representing persons, we represent not a multitude of variants of one and the same nature, or aspects of this nature; we represent concrete persons. Each one of them has a unique way of possessing the common human nature, which gives distinctive features to each: Peter, John, Paul.[19] The icon is linked to its prototype not because it is identical to that which it represents, which would be patently absurd. The icon is joined to its prototype because it portrays the person and carries his name. This is precisely what makes communion with the represented person possible, what makes him known. It is because of this connection that "the honor rendered to the image belongs to its prototype," according to the Fathers of the Seventh Ecumenical Council,[20] quoting the words of St Basil the Great (*On the Holy Spirit*, ch. 18). In their explanations, the Fathers often appeal to the comparison between the icon and the secular

18 *De fide orthodoxa, IV,* "De numero naturarum," PG 94: 1004A.
19 In Orthodoxy, the term "person" (ὑπόστασις) has an entirely different meaning from that used in contemporary language, where "person" is synonymous with "individual." For those interested in the Orthodox teaching on nature, person and grace, we recommend V. Lossky, *The Mystical Theology of the Eastern Church* (New York: St Vladimir's Seminary Press, 1976), and *In the Image and Likeness of God,* John H. Erickson and T. Bird, eds. (New York: St Vladimir's Seminary Press, 1985).
20 Mansi XIII, 324.

portrait: the emperor's portrait is the emperor; likewise, "the representation of Christ is Christ," and that of a saint is the saint. "If power is not divided or glory separated, then the honor given an image is given to the one portrayed in the image."[21]

To say this differently: if the iconoclasts saw only two possibilities—the identity of the two objects or the difference between them—for the Orthodox, on the other hand, even when there is a difference in nature, there is a certain link between the two objects, which can be simultaneously distinct and identical. The Persons of the Holy Trinity are distinct from one another, but they are consubstantial, that is, identical in nature. On the icon, on the other hand, there is a difference in nature and an identity of person. St Theodore the Studite expresses this as follows: "[In the Trinity], just as Christ differs from the Father by His person, so is Christ distinguished from His representation by nature."[22]

Having rejected the basis of Christian iconography, the image of Christ, the iconoclasts also naturally rejected all other icons. Once the icon of Christ has been rejected, they said, it is wrong to accept others, that is, icons of the Virgin and of the saints.

As we have already mentioned, the declaration of faith of the iconoclastic council, having modified Constantine Copronymus' point of view, speaks of the Virgin and of the saints with the greatest respect: "How dare one represent by means of pagan art," the council asks, "the Mother of God who is higher than the heavens and the saints" and "offend the saints who shine like the stars, with dead and gross material?" Even though iconoclasm began with such a declaration of deep veneration, in its normal, "organic" development, so to speak, it succeeded in denying the veneration of the Mother of God and of the saints. The Byzantine chronicler Theophanes asserts that Emperor Leo III already refused to venerate the Virgin and the saints, but this assertion is not confirmed by other sources. In any case, St John of Damascus, immediately responding to the imperial iconoclastic edict with his first apology *On the Divine Images*, foresaw very clearly where the rejection of icons would eventually lead. Responding to the rather moderate iconoclastic trend of this time, he

---

21 St John of Damascus, *De imaginibus oratio I*, PG 94: 1256A; *On the Divine Images*, trans. D. Anderson (New York: St Vladimir's Seminary Press, 1980), 36.

22 *Antirrheticus III*, ch. 3, par. 7, PG 99: 424A.

writes:

> If you make an image of Christ, and not of the saints, it is evident that you do not forbid images, but refuse to honor the saints... You are not waging war against images, but against the saints themselves.[23]

St John very clearly sees the intimate link that exists between the veneration of icons and that of the saints. The iconoclasts' refusal to venerate the saints naturally led to a denial of the veneration of their relics and, more generally, of all types of matter. For the Orthodox, by contrast, salvation is connected precisely with matter, since it is actualized in the hypostatic union of God with human flesh. Replying to the iconoclasts, St John of Damascus wrote: "I do not worship matter; I worship the Creator of matter who became matter for my sake, who willed to take His abode in matter; who worked out my salvation through matter."[24]

As we see, iconoclastic ideology was opposed to some of the most essential points of the teaching of the Orthodox Church. The very understanding that iconoclasts had of icons was diametrically opposed to the Orthodox understanding. This is why the two sides could not reach any agreement: They were speaking two different languages. As for the iconoclastic argument concerning the impossibility of representing Christ, it presents a pathetic attachment to "the ineffable" falsely understood, a dichotomy between "the spiritual" and "the sensory," an insufficient awareness of the reality of the Gospel story.[25]

In addition to the arguments of which we spoke, the iconoclasts formulated a whole series of other reasons against the veneration of icons. "There are no prayers," they said, "consecrating icons, making them into sacred objects. Thus, icons are not sacred objects: they are ordinary objects, having only the value conferred on them by the painter,"[26] that is, aesthetic, psychological, historical, and so forth.

The Fathers of the Seventh Ecumenical Council replied:

> Many objects we consider to be sacred are not sanctified by special prayers because they are full of holiness and grace in themselves. This is why we consider objects

---

23 *De imaginibus oratio I,* ch. 19, PG 94: 1249, *On the Divine Images,* trans. D. Anderson (New York: St Vladimir's Seminary Press, 1980), 26-7.
24 *Ibid.,* ch. 16, PG 94: 1245, trans., 23.
25 G. Florovsky, *The Byzantine Fathers of the V-VIII Centuries* (in Russian) (Paris, 1933); *The Defense of Holy Icons* (in Russian).
26 Sixth Session, Mansi XIII, 268ff.

of this kind to be worthy of veneration and why we kiss them. Thus, the vivifying cross itself, even though it is not sanctified by a special prayer, is considered to be worthy of veneration and is used as a means to gain sanctification. Therefore, the iconoclasts must either acknowledge the cross itself as an ordinary object, not worthy of veneration because it is not sanctified by a special prayer, or else they must also acknowledge the icon to be sacred and worthy of veneration.[27]

But the iconoclasts never ceased venerating the cross, which is quite an inconsistency, given their attitude towards icons.

Thus, according to the council Fathers, icons are full of grace because they are called sacred objects—"holy icons"—and because they contain grace. "Divinity is equally present in an image of the cross and in other divine objects," St Theodore the Studite says, "not by virtue of identity of nature, for these objects are not the flesh of God, but by virtue of their relative participation in divinity, for they participate in the grace and in the honor."[28] An icon is sanctified by the name of God and by the names of the friends of God, that is, of the saints, explains St John of Damascus,[29] and this is the reason why the icon receives the grace of the divine Spirit.[30]

In addition to their theological arguments, the iconoclasts also employed biblical and patristic argumentations. The most important, to which they returned ceaselessly, was the Old Testament prohibition. We have already seen how the Church understood the meaning of this proscription; there is no need to return to this now. The iconoclasts also said that nothing in the New Testament indicates that icons should be made or venerated. "The custom of making icons of Christ has no foundation either in the tradition of Christ, or in that of the apostles or the Fathers," they maintained.[31] "But," St Theodore the Studite replied,

nowhere did Christ order any word to be put down; and yet His image has been

---

27 *Ibid.*, 296D.
28 *Antirrheticus I*, ch. 10, PG 99: 340.
29 *De imaginibus oratio II*, ch. 14, PG 94(1): 1300.
30 The iconoclastic accusation, like the Orthodox response, proves that at the time of the Seventh Ecumenical Council the rite of the blessing of icons did not exist. This is very interesting for us, given our practice of blessing icons. In fact, the benediction rite is not always well understood by the Orthodox faithful. Frequently, they bring to church a painting with a religious theme, which in no way can be called an icon, and think that if the priest blesses it, it will become an icon. However, the benediction rite of an icon is not a magical formula. An image which is not an icon does not become an icon because it is blessed.
31 Sixth Session, Mansi XIII, 268B-C.

traced by the apostles and been preserved up to now. What is written down on paper and with ink, is put on the icon through various colors or another material.[32]

Ignoring the canons of the Quinisext Council, the iconoclasts asserted that the ecumenical councils had not given any instruction on this subject. In support of their position, they brought allegedly patristic texts. It must be said that in their argumentation, the iconoclasts frequently used dishonest methods. Thus, after the iconoclastic council of 754, they hid the texts which mentioned the story of the Holy Face, as we learn from the Acts of the Seventh Ecumenical Council. For the fifth session of this council, the *Acts* mention books which had been hidden by the iconoclasts and were produced at the council.[33]

In addition to the "Acts of the Apostles," a second-century gnostic apocryphon, the iconoclasts widely used the writings of Eusebius of Caesarea and St Epiphanius, a fourth-century bishop of Cyprus. The council Fathers viewed the first of these references as being well-founded; Eusebius, however, should not be considered as an authority in the Church on account of his leanings toward Arianism.

Regarding St Epiphanius, the Fathers of the council did not enter into his theology, but based themselves exclusively on the facts: on the one hand, there were texts written allegedly by St Epiphanius that supported his iconoclasm; there was, on the other hand, the undeniable fact that in Cyprus, where he was bishop, there were churches that had been decorated by paintings while he was still alive. Consequently, the Fathers viewed the writings attributed to St Epiphanius as spurious.[34]

32 *Antirrheticus I*, ch. 10, PG 99: 340D.
33 Mansi XIII, 169.
34 The question of the iconoclasm of St Epiphanius has always caused controversy. Thus, St Nicephorus, Patriarch of Constantinople, studied the writings in a work entitled *Against the Epiphanides*, and also in his refutations of the second iconoclastic council (*Adversus Epiphanidem*, ed. J. B. Pitra, *Spicilegium Solesmense* IV, 292ff). He arrives at the conclusion that they were falsified by the iconoclasts. St John of Damascus is less categorical: according to him, the work ascribed to St Epiphanius could have been written by someone else, other than the one whose name it carries, "which many people are in the habit of doing." Perhaps also, St John of Damascus continues, it was a matter not of iconoclasm, but of correcting abuses (*De imaginibus oratio I*, ch. 15, PG 94: 1257B-C). Modern scholarship is not unanimous on this question. Thus, K. Holl, in *Die Schriften gegen die Bilderverehrung* (1928), concludes that Epiphanius was an iconoclast. G. Ostrogorsky, in ch. 3 of *Studien zur Geschichte des byzantinischen Bilderstreites*, is of the opposite opinion. G. Florovsky, in *The Eastern Fathers of the Fourth Century* (in Russian) (New York, 1972), is almost certain that it is a matter of

In addition, the iconoclasts attributed to St Theodotus of Ancyra (fifth century) a text that was totally hostile to images but which he had in fact not written, something the Fathers also noticed. By dint of searching for texts, the iconoclasts managed to find an iconoclastic tendency even in St Basil the Great, whose veneration of images we have seen. "The lives of blessed men," St Basil wrote, "are in a certain way images of a life pleasing to God." From these words, the iconoclasts deduced that painted images were useless since there existed written images.[35]

The Seventh Ecumenical Council, which closes the first iconoclastic period, was held at Nicaea and opened on September 24. The acts of the council contain 307 signatures. The Pope of Rome, Hadrian I, sent two legates; the patriarchs of Alexandria and Antioch also sent their representatives, who brought a message from the Patriarch of Jerusalem expressing his approval of the restoration of the veneration of icons.

The council began with the acceptance, after public penitence, of eleven iconoclastic bishops into the Church. At the second meeting, two messages from Pope Hadrian I were read, one to the Patriarch of Constantinople, St Tarasius, the other to Emperor Constantine and his mother, the Empress Irene. The pope expressed his support for the veneration of icons and insisted on their necessity, but his confession of Orthodoxy amounted to a refutation of the accusation of idolatry. For the Eastern Church, then, this was a subject which had been left behind long ago, almost an anachronism. Quoting Scripture, the Pope referred to the tabernacle with the image of the cherubim. He then quoted a series of texts by Greek and Roman Fathers who, in his opinion, were in favor of icons, especially the one by Pope St Gregory I, which we already know, about the unlettered who should read on church walls what they cannot

iconoclastic interpolations, even for the story attributed to Epiphanius himself, which was later inserted into his writings. Florovsky is of the opinion that the writings of Epiphanius contained an implicit iconoclastic position, which he explains in terms of the fourth-century situation. For Epiphanius, "the transition from symbolism to realism in iconography could have seemed disturbing" (203). J. Meyendorff, in *Christ in Eastern Christian Thought* (New York, 1975), 135, believes that the authenticity of the incriminating fragments of Epiphanius is dubious. On the other hand, Th. Klauser, in *Die Äusserungen der alten Kirche zur Kunst, Gesammelte Arbeiten zur Liturgie-Geschichte* (Münster, 1974), 329-37, maintains their authenticity with certainty. On his part, Ch. Schönborn sees the same link between christology and iconoclasm in Eusebius and Epiphanius, "although less systematically justified in the latter" (*L'icône du Christ* [Freiburg, 1976], 77).

35 Sixth Session of the Sixth Council, Mansi XIII, 300A-B.

read in books. All this, for want of the christological arguments so important for the Church, could not have sounded very convincing either to the Orthodox or to the iconoclasts. But the opinion of the Pope of Rome, first in honor among the bishops, played an important role. It was respected; if not sufficiently founded, however, it jeopardized the Orthodox position or at least did not add effectively to the argumentation of the council. To give the message of the Pope more weight, the Greeks completed the quotation of St Gregory the Great—"The illiterate must read on church walls what they cannot read in books"— with the following precision: "and in this way, through the intermediary of images, those who gaze upon them ascend to faith, and to the recollection of salvation through the Incarnation of our Lord, Jesus Christ." Thus, they gave a christological basis to the reasoning of the Pope, and raised it to the level of the Byzantine theological discussions.[36] The text of the pontifical messages was also completed in passages that dealt with other questions raised by the Pope. Nonetheless, the two legates did not react against such rectifications, and declared at the council that the modified messages were indeed the ones they had brought.[37]

The Fathers then established the true doctrine of the veneration of icons. Their decisions are based primarily on Scripture. From the Old Testament they quoted Exodus 15:1 and 17-22, where Yahweh orders that the cherubim be placed in the tabernacle, and Numbers 7:88-9, where Yahweh speaks to Moses from among the cherubim. They also quoted the section from the vision of Ezekiel concerning the temple with the cherubim (Ez 3:16-20). From the New Testament, the Fathers cited Heb 9:1-5, a New Testament text on the tabernacle. Then followed the patristic declarations by St John Chrysostom, St Gregory of Nyssa, St Basil the Great, St Nilus of Sinai, and others we already know, as well as Canon 82 of the Quinisext Council.

Then the council was faced with the question of how icons should be venerated. Opinions were divided on this question. Some, such as the Patriarch of Constantinople, St Tarasius, believed that icons should be

---

36 It must be noted that, among the western writers, only Pope St Gregory II resorts to the dogma of the Incarnation in his apology for the image. Of Roman origin, he was greatly influenced by the East.

37 See G. Ostrogorsky, "Rom und Byzanz im Kampfe um die Bildererehrung," *Seminarium Kondakovianum* VI (Prague, 1933), 73-87.

venerated on the same level as sacred vessels. Others, such as the representatives of the Eastern patriarchs, maintained that images had the same importance as the cross, and that they should therefore be venerated equally with it. The council supported the latter.

Next, iconoclasm was condemned as a heresy. The Fathers concluded that iconoclasm, both in its theory and practice, recapitulated all the errors and heresies of the past: it was the sum total of a great number of heresies and errors. The iconoclasts were anathematized, and their works were confiscated. At the initiative of the legates of the Pope, an icon was placed in the middle of the cathedral of Hagia Sophia where the council had taken place; it was solemnly venerated by everyone.

It was declared that the iconoclastic council called together by Constantine Copronymus was not ecumenical, since the other local churches had not accepted it. Nor could it be called the "Seventh Council," since it was in disagreement with the six others, especially with the Quinisext Council, which the Fathers called the "Sixth Ecumenical Council." Sacred art, on the other hand, agreed with Christian dogmas; God Himself had sanctified it, since in the Old Testament he had designated men endowed by Him with special wisdom and knowledge to decorate the tabernacle.

Then followed a theological discussion which can be found in the Acts of the Council (sixth session). Here, the iconoclastic doctrine is explained point by point; as it is explained, the responses of the Church are given. We have already spoken of this in part.

The last two meetings were devoted to clarifying the final decisions, which are called the *Oros* of the council, and formulating the dogma of the veneration of icons. Here is the text:

> We retain, without introducing anything new, all the ecclesiastical traditions, written or not written, which have been established for us. One of these is the representation of painted images (εἰκονικῆς ἀναζωγραφήσεως), being in accord with the story of the biblical preaching, because of the belief in the true and non-illusory Incarnation of God the Word, for our benefit. For things which presuppose each other are mutually revelatory.
>
> Since this is the case, following the royal path and the teaching divinely inspired by our holy Fathers and the Tradition of the catholic Church—for we know that it is inspired by the Holy Spirit who lives in it—we decide in all correctness and after a thorough examination that, just as the holy and vivifying

cross, similarly the holy and precious icons painted with colors, made with little stones or with any other matter serving this purpose (ἐπιτηδείως), should be placed in the holy churches of God, on vases and sacred vestments, on walls and boards, in houses and on roads, whether these are icons of our Lord God and Savior, Jesus Christ, or of our spotless Sovereign Lady, the holy Mother of God, or of the holy angels and of holy and venerable men. For each time that we see their representation in an image, each time, while gazing upon them, we are made to remember the prototypes, we grow to love them more, and we are even more induced to worship them by kissing them and by witnessing our veneration (προσκύνησιν), not the true adoration (λατρείαν) which, according to our faith, is proper only to the one divine nature, but in the same way as we venerate the image of the precious and vivifying cross, the holy Gospel and other sacred objects which we honor with incense and candles according to the pious custom of our forefathers. For the honor rendered to the image goes to its prototype, and the person who venerates an icon venerates the person represented on it. Indeed, such is the teaching of our holy Fathers and the Tradition of the holy catholic Church which propagated the Gospel from one end of the earth to the other. Thus we follow Paul, who spoke in Christ, and the entire divine circle of apostles and all the holy Fathers who upheld the traditions which we follow. Thus, we prophetically sing the hymns of the victory of the Church: "Sing aloud, O daughter of Zion; shout, O Israel! Rejoice and exult with all your heart, O daughter of Jerusalem! The Lord has taken away the judgments against you, He has cast out your enemies. The King of Israel, the Lord, is in your midst; you shall fear evil no more" (Zeph 3:14-15).

Thus, we decide that those who dare to think or teach differently, following the example of the evil heretics; those who dare to scorn the ecclesiastical traditions, to make innovations or to repudiate something which has been sanctified by the Church, whether it be the Gospel or the representation of the cross, or the painting of icons, or the sacred relics of martyrs, or who have evil, pernicious and subversive feelings towards the traditions of the catholic Church; those, finally, who dare give sacred vases or venerable monasteries to ordinary uses: we decide that, if they are bishops or priests, they be defrocked; if they are monks or laymen, they be excommunicated.[38]

On several occasions in the conciliar decision, the Fathers refer to the Tradition or traditions of the Church. Thus, "retaining the established ecclesiastical traditions," the council made its decision according to the "teaching divinely inspired by the Fathers and the Tradition of the catholic Church." As we see, the Fathers of the council used the word "tradition" both in the plural ("the traditions of the catholic Church") and in

38 Mansi XIII, 377-80.

the singular ("the Tradition of the catholic Church"). This plural and singular correspond to the meaning given to the word "tradition" in each case.

Ecclesiastical traditions are the rules of faith passed on by the holy Fathers and retained by the Church. These are the various forms which externally convey the divine revelation, forms which are connected with the natural faculties and peculiarities of men—word, image, movement, custom. This includes the liturgical, iconographic, or other traditions.

In the latter case, the word "tradition," used in the singular, has a different meaning: it is the sacred Tradition of the Church, free from everything, not subordinate either to human faculties or idiosyncrasies. "The true and holy Tradition," says Metropolitan Philaret of Moscow, "is not simply the visible and verbal tradition of the teachings, canons, ceremonies, and rituals, but it is also the invisible and actual instruction by grace and sanctification."[39] The concept of Tradition can, in this case, be defined as the life of the Holy Spirit in the Church, giving every member of the Body of Christ the ability to learn, see and recognize the truth in its own light, and not in the light of human intelligence. It is the true knowledge created in man by the divine light which "has shone in our hearts to enlighten them with the knowledge of God's glory" (2 Cor 4:6). In other words, Tradition is the ability to know the truth in the Holy Spirit, the communication of "the Spirit of Truth" who actualizes the fundamental power of the Church: its awareness of the revealed truth, its ability, in the light of the Holy Spirit, to discern and determine what is true and what is false. Only by living in the Tradition can we say: "It has been decided by the Holy Spirit and by ourselves" (Acts 15:38).[40] This Tradition lives and is communicated in the different forms of ecclesiastic traditions, one of which is precisely iconography, as the Fathers of the Seventh Ecumenical Council said.

By referring to the Tradition of the Church, the council showed that the basis for the existence of icons is not Holy Scripture (the lack of indications in it about icons had been evoked by the iconoclasts), but

39 As quoted by G. Florovsky, *Ways of Russian Theology*, Part One, trans. R. L. Nichols (Belmont, Mass., 1979), 214.

40 On this subject, see the article entitled "Tradition and Traditions," by V. Lossky in L. Ouspensky and V. Lossky, *The Meaning of Icons* (New York: St Vladimir's Seminary Press, 1982), 11-22.

Holy Tradition. Scripture itself was written according to Tradition; during the first decades of its existence, the Church did not yet have Scripture, and lived according to Tradition. As is known, modern Protestantism sees in Scripture the only expression of revelation. But, as the decision of the council states, the revealed truths communicated by the Holy Spirit in the Tradition of the Church are not limited to the written tradition. Even those things which had been accomplished by Christ during His life on earth are not limited to what we know from Scripture: "There was much else Jesus did; if it were written down in detail, I do not suppose the world itself would hold all the books that would be written" (Jn 2:25). St John of Damascus adds:

> The apostles passed on many things without having them written down. The Apostle of the Gentiles is a witness to this: "Stand firm, then, brothers, and keep the traditions that we taught you, whether by mouth or by letter" (2 Thess 2:15). And to the Corinthians, he writes: "I congratulate you for remembering me so consistently and for maintaining the traditions as I passed them on to you" (1 Cor 11:2).[41]

Thus, iconography is part of the Tradition of the Church. By preserving it, "We follow Paul...and the whole divine circle of Apostles," because the tradition of making painted images existed already in the time of apostolic preaching, in the same way as we see it in the teachings of the holy Fathers and historians who witness to this fact in the writings which have been preserved.[42]

In other words, iconography is a means that has existed from the beginning of Christianity to express the Tradition, a way of conveying divine revelation. By renouncing one of the traditions (iconography), iconoclasm distorted the sacred Tradition of the Church.

Authentic, sacred Tradition is possible only in the Church, which is the perpetuation of Pentecost; that is, it is possible only in the Church in which the grace of the Holy Spirit, who reveals the truth and strengthens

41 *De fide orthodoxa*, IV, ch. 16, PG 94: 1173, 1176. To this reference John of Damascus makes to St Paul could be added that, if Christianity were limited to Scripture only, one would have to arrive at the clearly absurd conclusion that most of the apostles did not fulfill the highest commandment of the Lord to proclaim the good news throughout the world, to all of creation. Indeed, in addition to the twelve apostles, Christ had sixty-six others. All that remains in written form is four Gospels, a few Epistles, and the Acts of the Apostles. But what has not been put down in Scripture continues to live in the Church Tradition, especially in the liturgy and in iconography.

42 Sixth Session, Mansi XIII, 252.

us in it, flows uninterruptedly. Instructed by the Holy Spirit who lives in the Church, the council proclaimed the dogma of the veneration of icons. The icon must be an object of our veneration, not of the true adoration (λατρεία) which belongs only to God, but precisely the veneration (προσκύνησις) which we show to the Cross and the Gospel; in other words, we must venerate the visible image in the same way as we do the verbal image and other objects.

The veneration of the Gospel and of the Cross has never been formulated dogmatically because it was never questioned either in the Church or among the heretics. But as far as the image is concerned, the Church had to substantiate dogmatically the well-foundedness of the very existence of the image and of its veneration.

The council, therefore, maintained that the icon, like Scripture, helps to "prove the true and non-imaginary Incarnation of God the Word." Here we find, expressed and confirmed, a fact we already know from Canon 82 of the Quinisext Council: that the icon is based on the Incarnation. It is used to refute all kinds of abstract ideas about the Incarnation, together with the errors and heresies engendered by such ideas.

The council states that Holy Scripture and the holy image are "mutually revelatory." One single content is witnessed in two different ways—with words or with images—conveying the same revelation in the light of the same sacred and living Tradition of the Church. We read in the council's canons:

> The Fathers neither transmitted to us that it was necessary to read the Gospel nor did they convey to us that it was necessary to make icons. But if they conveyed the one, they also conveyed the other, because a representation is inseparable from the biblical account, and, *vice versa,* the biblical account is inseparable from a representation. Both are right and worthy of veneration because they explain one another and, indisputably, substantiate one another.[43]

Thus, the visible image is equivalent to the verbal image. Just as the word of Scripture is an image, so is the painted image a word. "That which the word communicates by sound, a painting demonstrates silently by representation," the Fathers of the council said, referring to St Basil the Great. Elsewhere they write, "By means of these two ways which complement

43 *Ibid.,* 296A.

one another, that is, by reading and by the visible image, we gain knowledge of the same thing."[44] In other words, the icon contains and proclaims the same truth as the Gospel. Like the Gospel and the Cross, it is one of the aspects of divine revelation and of our communion with God, a form in which the union of divine and human activity, synergy, is accomplished. Aside from their direct meaning, the sacred image as well as the Gospel are reflections of the heavenly world; the one and the other are symbols of the Spirit they contain. Thus, both the one and other transmit concrete, specific realities, not human ideas. In other words, what was asked was "How can the icon correspond to the Gospel and explain it, and *vice versa*?"

In the eyes of the Church, therefore, the icon is not art illustrating Holy Scripture; it is a language that corresponds to it and is equivalent to it, corresponding not to the letter of Scripture or to the book itself as an object, but to the evangelical *kerygma*, that is, to the content of the Scripture itself, to its meaning, as is true also for liturgical texts. This is why the icon plays the same role as Scripture does in the Church; it has the same liturgical, dogmatic, and educational meaning.[45]

The content of holy Scripture is conveyed by the icon not in the form of a theoretical instruction, but in a liturgical manner, that is, in a living way, appealing to all the human faculties. In it, the truth contained in Scripture is conveyed in light of the entire spiritual experience of the Church, of its Tradition. It therefore corresponds to Scripture in the same way as the liturgical texts correspond to it, as we have said. Indeed, these texts do not merely reproduce Scripture as such: they are interwoven with it. By alternating and juxtaposing passages, they reveal their meaning and show us how to live the biblical preaching. By representing various moments of sacred history, the icon visibly conveys their meaning, their *vital* significance. Thus, Scripture lives in the Church and in each of its members both through the liturgy and through the icon. This is why the unity of the liturgical image and of the liturgical word is of crucial importance, because the two modes of expression control one another.

44 *Ibid.*, 300C.

45 It should be noted that the image has certain possibilities which the word does not have: it is a more direct form of expression, it has a better capacity for conveying general ideas than the word. Thus, an icon portrays directly and concisely that which is expressed in the entire liturgy of a feast.

They live the same life; in worship, they share a common, constructive action. The denial of one of these modes of expression leads to the downfall of the other. What happened among the iconoclasts of the eighth and ninth centuries—a total decline of the liturgical and therefore of the spiritual life—was the result of a repudiation of the sacred image.

To replace icons, the iconoclasts intensified preaching, religious poetry, and they introduced all types of music. On this subject, Pope St Gregory II wrote to Emperor Leo III: "You have entertained the people with vain discourses, futile words, citharas, castanets, flutes, with inaneness; instead of doxologies and thanksgivings, you have led the people into fables."[46] This is how the liturgical tradition was broken, with everything it entailed. Indeed, the divine revelation penetrates into the believing people through the liturgy and the icon, sanctifying life, giving things their true meaning, and thus becomes the fundamental task to be fulfilled by the faithful.

Quoting the words of St Basil the Great, the Seventh Ecumenical Council asserts that "the honor rendered to the image passes to its prototype, for the person who venerates an icon venerates the person represented on it." Thus, icons are intermediaries between the represented persons and the praying faithful, causing them to commune in grace. In church during the liturgy, the faithful, through the intermediary of icons and liturgical prayers, enter into communion with the heavenly Church, forming with it a single whole. In its liturgy, the Church is one. It includes in its fullness the angels and men, the living and the dead, and finally, all of creation. And when the priest incenses the church, he embraces in his movement both the saints represented on icons and the faithful gathered in the church, thus expressing the unity of the earthly and heavenly Church.

Thus, sacred art is liturgical by its very nature, not only because it serves as a framework for the liturgy and makes it complete, but because it corresponds to it perfectly. Being therefore an art of worship, the icon has never "served" religion in the sense in which art historians sometimes understand it,[47] that is, as an auxiliary element borrowed from outside

---

46 Second message, Mansi XII, 978B.
47 "Icons are in no way an integral part, especially not an essential part, of Orthodox worship" (H. G. Beck, *Von der Fragwürdigkeit der Ikonen*, Bayerische Akademie der Wissenschaften,

and used by the Church. The icon, like the word, is an integral part of religion: it is a way of knowing God, one of the means of contacting Him. Just like the image of the precious and lifegiving Cross, which is the distinctive sign of Christianity, its standard, so to speak, the icon is a confession of the truth, a profession of faith.

The decisions of the Seventh Ecumenical Council were signed by representatives of the entire Church, including the Roman Church. Having received the canons of the council, Pope Hadrian I had them translated into Latin. This translation was so inaccurate and crude that Anastasius the Librarian, a ninth-century Roman scholar, declared that it was absolutely unreadable, and wrote another one. But the first translation had unfortunate consequences and caused many misunderstandings, particularly the moderate iconoclasm of Charlemagne. One of the main blunders in this translation concerns the dogma of the veneration of icons itself, the prpoer attitude toward the sacred image. Wherever the Greek had used the word προσκύνησις, the Latin used the word *adoratio*. But προσκύνησις means "veneration" and not "adoration," and the council specified and especially emphasized that the correct attitude toward the image should be one of honor and veneration, not that of true adoration (λατρεία), which befits God alone.[48] What is really tragic is not just this translation, but the fact that it was taken seriously in the West, and that no one was aware of its absurdity.

Charlemagne, to whom the Pope had sent the canons of the Seventh Ecumenical Council (in their Latin translation), was outraged by what he saw. He made a stormy protest to Hadrian I, and, in response to what he believed to be the canons of the council, sent to the Pope a document called the *Libri Carolini*, which had been written by his Frankish theologians. Let us give a few examples of the way in which these theologians "understood" the Acts of the Seventh Ecumenical Council.

To the iconoclasts who claimed that only the Eucharist was the true

Sitzungsberichte [1975], No. 7 [München, 1975], 33).

48 "The distinction was never well understood in the West," John Meyendorff notes in *Christ in Eastern Christian Thought* (New York: St Vladimir's Seminary Press, 1975); he adds that "St Thomas Aquinas himself admitted a 'relative adoration' (*latria*) of the images, and this provoked accusations against the Latin Church by certain Orthodox [the Council of St Sophia, in 1450] (Mansi XXXII, 103), and later by the Reformers of the Sixteenth Century" (141).

image of Christ, the council had answered that neither Christ nor the Apostles nor the Fathers had ever called the eucharistic gifts images, but had called them the true Body and Blood of Christ. Not understanding either the iconoclastic assertion or the Orthodox response, the Frankish theologians wrote in response to the Seventh Ecumenical Council:

> It is absurd and rash to place icons and the Eucharist on the same level and to say that just as the fruits of the earth [that is, bread and wine] are transformed into a mystery worthy of our veneration, similarly images are transformed into the veneration shown to the person represented on these images.

As can be seen, this is sheer nonsense. Héfélé, the church historian, comments on this in his *Histoire des Conciles*: "The Council of Nicaea did not say this, nor anything like it."[49] Pope Hadrian I had to explain in his answer that it was not the Fathers of the council, but the iconoclasts who had confused the Eucharist with the image.

But what was most important was not this bad translation: it was the fundamental difference in attitude toward the icon that existed between the Greek and the Frankish theologians, their different way of understanding the meaning and aim of the sacred image. Thus we read in the *Libri Carolini*: "They [that is, the Greeks] place almost all their hope in icons, while we venerate the saints in their body, or, rather, in their relics or clothing, following the tradition of the ancient Fathers." But the Greeks did not show any preference to icons over relics; they only placed each in its place. "The icon cannot be placed on the same level as the cross, the sacred vases, or the Holy Scriptures," the *Libri Carolini* continue, since in the mind of their creators, "images are only the product of the artists' imagination."[50]

The misunderstandings between the Fathers of the council and the Frankish theologians were not limited to the examples we have mentioned. It can be said that at the moment when the Seventh Ecumenical Council developed the theology of the sacred image, "at that very moment, the *Libri Carolini* poisoned Western art at its source."[51] Not only did the *Libri* deprive the sacred image of its dogmatic basis, but, by handing it over to the imagination of the artists, they deviated even from the attitude of St Gregory the Great, which was already an anachronism

49 Héfélé, *Histoire des Conciles*, vol. 3, Part 2, 1073.
50 Bk 2, ch. 26, Héfélé, *ibid.*, 1073.
51 Paul Evdokimov, *L'art sacré*, nos 9-10 (Paris, 1953), 20.

at the time of iconoclasm. Their attitude, which was also that of Charlemagne, may be summarized as follows: Icons should not be destroyed, nor should they be venerated. In justifying the existence of the icon against the iconoclasts, the West did not even understand the essence of the debate that was raging in Byzantium. What was, for the Byzantines, a matter of life and death, passed unnoticed in the West. This is why Charlemagne won the discussion with Hadrian I: the Pope had to give in.

In 794 Charlemagne called together a council in Frankfurt. Consisting of more than 300 bishops, this council did not go as far as the *Libri Carolini* and did not proscribe the veneration of icons in favor of relics. But it rejected both the iconoclastic council of 754 and the Seventh Ecumenical Council, saying that

> neither one nor the other deserves the title of "seventh." Believing in the Orthodox doctrine which states that images should only be used to decorate churches, and in memory of past canons according to which we should adore only God and venerate the saints, we do not want to prohibit images as does one of these councils or to adore them as does the other, and we reject the writings of this ridiculous council.[52]

The absurdity of the whole situation is clear: the Seventh Ecumenical Council forbids the adoration of icons, and the Council of Frankfurt is indignant because it decrees such adoration. But what is most absurd is that the legates of the same Pope Hadrian I, who had signed the decisions of the Seventh Ecumenical Council, also signed the decisions of the Council of Frankfurt.

After the Council of Frankfurt, another council was held in Paris in 825. This council also condemned the Seventh Ecumenical Council. Soon after the Council of Paris, both Bishops Claudius of Turin and Agobard of Lyons attacked images. Iconoclasm reached its peak in the West when Bishop Claudius also began attacking the veneration of the cross, which even the most impassioned iconoclasts in Byzantium had been afraid to do.[53]

Thus, though the Council of Frankfurt approved of the use of icons, it did not see any dogmatic or liturgical importance in them. It considered them to be "decorations in churches" and, furthermore, as "a memory of

52 Héfélé, *op. cit.*, 1068.
53 L. Bréhier, *L'art chrétien* (Paris, 1928), 196.

past canons." It is significant that the Roman Church, even though it recognizes the Seventh Ecumenical Council, has in effect remained in the same position as the Council of Frankfurt, and this is why the image, which for the Orthodox is a language of the Church, an expression of the divine revelation and an integral part of its worship, never played this role in the Church of Rome. It is true that, at the time of Charlemagne, it still remained faithful to Orthodoxy. For more than thirty years (at least between the Council of Frankfurt in 794 and that of Paris in 825), the local churches of Charlemagne's empire and of his successor Louis the Pious were, on the question of icons, openly opposed to the catholic doctrine and to the mother church in Rome. This opposition disappeared only gradually:[54] eventually, the Church of Rome was obliged to accept the principle advocated in the *Libri Carolini* and by the Council of Frankfurt, and it ended up following the road of innovation by distancing itself from the decisions of the Seventh Council.

If we view the present situation, in a world which calls itself Christian, in the light of the closing words of the *oros* of this council—"those who dare...to make innovations, or to repudiate something which has been sanctified by the Church, whether it be the Gospel or the representation of the cross, or the painting of icons, or the sacred relics of martyrs..." we will see that only the Orthodox Church has remained faithful to this decision. As to the non-Orthodox world, some have repudiated what has been sanctified by the Church, such as the Protestants who refuse to venerate icons or saints' relics; others, like the Roman Catholics, have followed the road of innovations.

The final toll of iconoclasm was heavy. During that period, everything that could be destroyed was destroyed, and this is why we have so few icons from the early centuries. "Wherever there were images," a contemporary says, "they were destroyed by fire or thrown to the ground, or effaced with a coating." "Those that were in mosaic," another one states, "were ripped down; those that had been painted with colored wax were scraped off. All beauty disappeared from the churches."[55] State servants were sent to the most remote provinces to find and destroy works of sacred art. A great

54 See Bolotov, *History of the Church During the Period of the Ecumenical Councils*, III (in Russian) (Petrograd, 1918), 586.
55 Quoted by Ch. Diehl, *Manuel d'art byzantin*, vol. 1 (Paris, 1926), 365.

number of Orthodox were executed, imprisoned and tortured, and their properties were confiscated. Others were banished or exiled to faraway provinces. In short, it was a real catastrophe. Before iconoclasm, the Orthodox often had no clear awareness of the importance of sacred art. But the violence of the persecution and the steadfastness of the confessors in venerating icons emphasized once and for all the importance of the sacred image. In spite of all persecutions and cruelties, despite the iconoclastic imperial decrees signed by the patriarchs, despite the number of iconoclast bishops (338 at the council of 754), despite the anathemas they pronounced against those who venerated, painted or possessed icons—the believing people never renounced their veneration. Neither the monks, who comprised the vanguard of the Church, nor the simple believers accepted blindly what could have seemed like censorship by the Church, for they knew what the Church can accept and what it cannot. "[Our] aim," John of Damascus wrote, "is to raise a hand which fights for the truth."[56] In the heat of battle, the Church found words capable of expressing the richness and depth of its teaching. Its profession constitutes a treasure we have inherited, one which is of particular importance to our time.

The catastrophe of iconoclasm demanded a supreme effort, a gathering of the energies of the Church, the blood of its martyrs and confessors, the spiritual experience and wisdom of the apologist Fathers, the steadfastness and audacity of the bishops who remained faithful to Orthodoxy. This was truly a collective effort of the Church.

What was at stake in this struggle was neither art nor the didactic and decorative function of the icon, nor was it a matter of some theological "superstructure" or a discussion about ritual, about a mere Christian usage.[57] What was at stake was the true profession of the dogma of the Incarnation, and therefore of Christian anthropology. "It was a specifically dogmatic debate, and theological depths were revealed by it."[58]

The dogma of the divine Incarnation has two essential aspects: "God became man so that man might become God." On the one hand, God comes into the world and participates in its history, "dwells among us";

56　*De imaginibus oratio I*, ch. 3, PG 94:1233, trans. D. Anderson, *On the Divine Images*, 14.

57　H. G. Beck sees in this only "eine Frage christlicher Praxis" (a question of Christian practice), *Von der Fragwürdigkeit der Ikone, op. cit.*, 44.

58　G. Florovsky, *The Byzantine Fathers* (in Russian), *op. cit.*, 247.

on the other hand, there is the purpose and meaning of this Incarnation: the divinization of man and, through this, the transformation of all creation, the building up of the Kingdom of God. In this world, the Church is the incipient "Kingdom to come": such is the reason for its existence. This is why everything in the Church converges toward this goal—all of life, all activity, every manifestation of human creativity, including artistic creation.

But iconoclasm, both in its teaching and in its practices, undermined the saving mission of the Church at its foundation. In theory, it did not deny the dogma of the Incarnation. On the contrary, the iconoclasts justified their hatred of the icon by claiming to be profoundly faithful to this dogma. But in reality, the opposite happened: by denying the human image of God, they consequently denied the sanctification of matter in general. They disavowed all human holiness and even denied the very possibility of sanctification, the deification of man. In other words, by refusing to accept the consequences of the Incarnation—the sanctification of the visible, material world—iconoclasm undermined the entire economy of salvation. "The one who thinks as you do," St George of Cyprus said in a discussion with an iconoclast bishop, "blasphemes against the Son of God and does not confess His economy accomplished in the flesh."[59] Through the denial of the image, Christianity became an abstract theory; it became disincarnate, so to speak; it was led back to the ancient heresy of Docetism, which had been refuted a long time before. It is therefore not surprising that iconoclasm was linked to a general secularization of the Church, a de-sacralization of all aspects of its life. The Church's own domain, its inner structure, was invaded by a secularized power. Churches were assaulted with secular images, worship was deformed by mundane music and poetry. This is why the Church, in defending the icon, defended not only the foundation of the Christian faith, the divine Incarnation, but, at the same time, the very meaning of its existence. It fought against its disintegration in the elements of this world. "Not only the destiny of Christian art was at stake, but 'Orthodoxy' itself."[60]

59 Quoted by G. Ostrogorsky, "The Works of the Orthodox Apologists" (in Russian), *Seminarium Kondakovianum*, I (Prague, 1927), 46.

60 G. Florovsky, "Origen, Eusebius, and the Iconoclastic Controversy," *Church History* 19 (1950) 79. See also, G. Ladner, "Der Bilderstreit und die Kunstlehren der byzantinischen und abendländischen Theologie," *Zeitschrift für Kirchengeschichte* 50 (1931); "Origin and Significance of the Byzantine Iconoclastic Controversy," *Medieval Studies* II (1940); P. Lukas Koch, "Zur Theologie der Christus-Ikone," *Benediktinische Monatschrift*, Beuron 19 (1937) 11-12; 20 (1938) 1-2, 5-6, 7-8.

14. *Christ Pantocrator* (All-powerful/almighty)
Russian icon of the 16th century
Photo: Temple Gallery, London

The dogmatic foundations of the content of the icon were developed by generations of Fathers fighting against the heterodox christology and anthropology of the preceding centuries. We can only make Chr. von Schönborn's conclusion our own:

> The christological debates lasted for centuries. During all these years, the Church never ceased to confess the mystery revealed and sealed in the Holy Face of Jesus Christ, the consubstantial image of the Father [Nicaea I], the Word become flesh without change [Ephesus], true God and true Man [Chalcedon], One of the Trinity who came to suffer for us [Constantinople II], the Word of God whose human will and activity, in perfect harmony with the divine plan, consented to suffer until death [Constantinople III]. After viewing these turbulent centuries, these terrible, distressing struggles around the true confession of Christ, our gaze stops and settles on an image that is silent and serene: the icon of Christ [Fig. 14].[61]

What lay at the basis of the iconoclastic attitude towards the icon and everything related to it was not the Old Testament proscription, despite the importance this argument had at the beginning of the conflict. Certainly, iconoclasm was born in the East and has often been characterized as being marked by a Semitic mentality, by an Eastern, magical conception of the image.[62] All this may have played its role in certain iconoclastic circles. However, the heresy itself has much deeper roots, as the most pertinent studies have shown, namely those of G. Florovsky. As an Orthodox theologian, having studied the origins of iconoclasm, this author concludes that the current interpretation, all too often repeated, must be reversed. The main inspiration of iconoclastic thought was hellenistic, and this heresy was actually a return to pre-Christian Hellenism.[63] Florovsky views the entire conflict as a new phase in an age-long process: In the eighth-ninth century conflict, the iconoclasts represented an unreformed and uncompromising position, of an Origenistic and Platonic trend.[64] At this time, Origenism, condemned by the Fifth Ecumenical Council, was far from being a settled question. It was a trend of

---

61   Christoph von Schönborn, *L'icône du Christ. Fondements théologiques* (Freiburg, 1976), 134. This is where one has to see the true and profound meaning of the statement, so often and so differently commented upon, of the Fathers of the Seventh Ecumenical Council, according to which sacred art depended on the holy Fathers, and the artistic aspect depended only on the artist (Mansi XIII, 252C).

62   See G. Ostrogorsky, "The Works of the Orthodox Apologists," *op. cit.*, 36.

63   "We should not forget," the same author adds, "that...the iconoclastic cause was popular in the hellenized quarters, in the court circles, and in the army, whereas in the lower classes it never had flourished," "Origen, Eusebius," *op. cit.*, 83.

64   *Ibid.*, 96.

thought that was still very much alive, and the symbolic-allegorical method of its reasoning could not have been more favorable to the argumentation of iconoclastic theology. Actually, it marked a return to the ancient dichotomy between matter and spirit. In such a system, an image can only be an obstacle to spirituality: not only is it made of matter, but it also represents the body, which is matter. Origen's christology was the backdrop and the premise for the argumentation of his zealous disciple Eusebius of Caesarea, as it is found in his letter to Constantia, the sister of Emperor Constantine. When she wanted to obtain an icon of Christ, Eusebius explained that an image representing His historical aspect would be a regression, since the body of the Lord was transformed, at present, into an unutterable glory. Only in spirit could one contemplate the glory in which Christ finds Himself after his Ascension; only pagans try to represent the unrepresentable.

Indeed, here we find the difficulty the ancient world had in accepting and assimilating the Christian revelation in its fullness—a difficulty which lay at the root of all the heresies and which has never been removed, nor could it be. Indeed, did not St Irenaeus, well before Origenistic intellectualism, already struggle to safeguard the integrity of the Christian revelation in its bodily manifestation? Chr. von Schönborn is right in showing the evolution of a christology infected by the hellenistic heritage, beginning with Arius, which had to lead inevitably to this conflict between Origenistic symbolism and the historicity of the Gospel. This is why "wherever a polemic against the Christian image starts, it is all too often based on a questionable theological vision (Eusebius, Epiphanius, Asterius of Amasea, the Montanist Tertullian of *De Pudicitia*)," as Schönborn notes.[65] Let us repeat that on the eve of the conflict, the Quinisext Council, which eliminated symbols, had in mind symbolism as a principle, "the pagan immaturity" represented by "Origen, Didymus and Evagrius who restored Greek fables" (Canon 1 of the council).

Iconoclasm closes the series of great heresies of the christological period. Every one of them struck a blow at one or another aspect of the divine economy, at the salvation resulting from the Incarnation of God. Iconoclasm, however, no longer attacked a particular aspect, but the economy of salvation as a whole. Just as this very complex heresy represented a general

65 Von Schönborn, *L'icône du Christ, op. cit.*, 84, note.

assault on Orthodox teaching, so was the reestablishment of the veneration of icons not merely a single victory, but the victory of Orthodoxy as such. The Church triumphed, and will continue to triumph over a multitude of heresies. But one of its victories, that over iconoclasm, has been solemnly proclaimed as the Triumph of Orthodoxy as such.

10

The Meaning and Content of the Icon

The meaning and the content of the icon arise from the teaching the Church formulated in answering iconoclasm.

The dogmatic foundation of the veneration of icons and the meaning and content of the liturgical image are particularly revealed by the liturgy of two feast days: that of the Holy Face, which we have already mentioned, and that of the Triumph of Orthodoxy, which is the feast of the victory of the icon and of the ultimate triumph of the dogma of the divine Incarnation.

The basis for our study will be the kontakion of the Triumph of Orthodoxy, which is a true verbal icon of the feast. This text, which is of an extraordinary richness and depth, expresses all of the Church's teaching about images. It is believed that the text dates to no earlier than the tenth century, but it is possible that it is contemporary with the canon of the feast. If this is the case, it dates to the ninth century, that is, to the very moment of the Triumph of Orthodoxy. The canon was, in fact, written by St Theophanes the Marked, a confessor of Orthodoxy during the second iconoclastic period. St Theophanes eventually became Metropolitan of Nicaea and died ca. 847. This canon is therefore written by a man who personally participated in the struggle to preserve the icon. It represents the totality of the Church's experience, a concrete and real experience of divine revelation, an experience defended with blood. On the occasion of the triumph of the icon, it expresses in a concise, exact form, in a few sentences, the entire economy of salvation, and thereby the teaching on the image and its content.

No one could describe the Word of the Father;
But when He took flesh from you, O Theotokos,
He consented to be described,
And restored the fallen image to its former state by uniting it to divine beauty.
We confess and proclaim our salvation in word and images.

The first part of the kontakion tells of the abasement of the second person of the Holy Trinity, and thus, of the christological basis of the icon. The words which follow reveal the meaning of the Incarnation, the accomplishment of the divine plan for man and consequently for the universe. It can be said that these two phrases illustrate the patristic formula: "God became man so that man might become God." The end of the kontakion expresses man's answer to God, his confession of the saving truth of the Incarnation, his acceptance of the divine economy and his participation in the work of God and, therefore, the achievement of his salvation: "We confess and proclaim our salvation in word and images."

The first part of the kontakion ("No one could describe the Word of the Father; but when He took flesh from you, O Theotokos...") can be summarized in the following way: The second person of the Holy Trinity becomes man and yet remains what He is, that is, fully God, possessing the fullness of divine nature, hence uncircumscribable in His divinity, for "no one could describe the Word of the Father." God assumes the human nature which He created; He borrows the human nature in its totality from the Mother of God; and, without changing His divinity, without confusing it with humanity, He becomes God and Man at the same time. "The Word became flesh so that the flesh could become word," according to St Mark the Ascetic.[1] This is the humiliation, the *kenosis* of God; He who is absolutely inaccessible to man, who is indescribable and un-representable, becomes describable and representable by assuming human flesh. The icon of Jesus Christ, the God-Man, is an expression of the dogma of Chalcedon in image; indeed, it represents the person of the Son of God who became man, who by His divine nature is consubstantial with the Father and by His human nature is consubstantial with us, "similar to us in everything except sin," in the expression of Chalcedon. During His life on earth, Christ reunited in Himself the image of God and the image of the servant about whom St Paul speaks (Phil 2:6-7). The men who surrounded Christ saw Him only as a man, albeit often as a prophet. For the unbelievers, His divinity is hidden by His form of a servant. For them, the Savior of the world is only a historical figure, the man Jesus. Even His most beloved disciples saw Christ only once in His glorified, deified humanity, and not in the form of a servant; this was before the passion, at

---

1 "Epistle to the Monk Nicholas," *Russian Philokalia*, vol. 1, 420.

the moment of His transfiguration on Mount Tabor. But the Church has "eyes to see" just as it has "ears to hear." This is why it hears the word of God in the Gospel, which is written in human words. Similarly, it always considers Christ through the eyes of the unshakeable faith in His divinity. This is why the Church depicts Him in icons not as an ordinary man, but as the God-Man in His glory, even at the moment of His supreme humiliation. We shall examine later how the Church does this. Here it is only necessary to note that this is precisely the reason why, in its icons, the Orthodox Church never represents Christ simply as a man who suffers physically, as is the case in western religious art.

The image of the God-Man was precisely what the iconoclasts could not understand. They asked how the *two natures* of Christ could be represented. But the Orthodox did not even think of representing either the *divine nature* or the *human nature* of Christ. They represented His person, the person of the God-Man who unites in Himself the two natures without confusion or division.

It is characteristic that the kontakion of the Triumph of Orthodoxy is addressed not to one of the persons of the Holy Trinity, but to the Mother of God. This shows the unity in the Church's teaching about Christ and the Mother of God. The Incarnation of the second person of the Trinity is the fundamental dogma of Christianity, but the confession of this dogma is possible only by confessing the Virgin Mary to be the true Mother of God. Indeed, if the negation of the human image of God logically leads to the negation of the very meaning of our salvation, the opposite is also true: the existence and the veneration of the icon of Christ implies the importance of the Mother of God, whose consent, "let it be to me according to Thy word" (Lk 1:38), was the indispensable condition for the Incarnation, and who alone permitted God to become visible and therefore representable. According to the Fathers, the representation of the God-Man is based precisely on the representable humanity of His Mother. "Since Christ was born of the indescribable Father," explains St Theodore the Studite,

He cannot have an image. Indeed, what image could correspond to the divinity whose representation is absolutely forbidden by Holy Scripture? But from the moment Christ is born of a describable mother, He naturally has an image which corresponds to that of His mother. If He could not be represented by art, this would mean that He was not born of a representable mother, but that He was born only of the Father, and that He was not incarnate. But this contradicts the whole divine economy of our salvation.[2]

This possibility of representing the God-Man in the flesh which He borrowed from His mother is contrasted by the Seventh Ecumenical Council with the absolute impossibility of representing God the Father. The Fathers of the council repeat the authoritative argument of Pope St Gregory II, contained in his letter to the Emperor Leo III the Isaurian:

Why do we neither describe nor represent the Father of the Lord Jesus Christ? Because we do not know what He is...And if we had seen and known Him as we have seen and known His Son, we would have tried to describe Him and to represent Him in art.[3]

The reasoning of this council, as well as the words of St Theodore the Studite, touch upon a subject that is very relevant and of great dogmatic importance, that is, the representation of God the Father in church practice. Human thought has not always measured up to real theology, as artistic creation has not always been equal to authentic iconography. Among other errors, we often find the image of God the Father. This image has been particularly widespread in the Orthodox Church since the seventeenth century. It will be necessary to return to this question later and to analyze it in more detail, in respect to the prohibition of the image of God the Father by the Great Council of Moscow in 1666-67. There-fore, we will limit ourselves here simply to several general considerations regarding the texts which we have quoted.

As we see, the Seventh Ecumenical Council speaks of the absence of the image of God the Father, who is not incarnate and is consequently invisible and non-representable. The council thus emphasizes the differ-ence between the representability of the Son, because He is incarnate, and the absolute impossibility of representing the Father. We have every right to conclude from this that, from the doctrinal point of view, the council confirms this impossibility of representing God the Father. Obviously, anything can be represented, since the human imagination has no limit. But the fact is that everything is not representable. Many things concern-ing God are not only not representable in image and not describable by words, but are even positively inconceivable to man. It is precisely because of this inconceivable, unknowable character of God the Father that the

2   *Antirrheticus I*, ch. 2, PG 99: 417C.
3   Mansi XII, 963E.

council proclaims the impossibility of making His image. We have only one way of knowing the Holy Trinity. We know the Father by the Son ("He who sees Me, sees Him who sent Me," we read in Jn 12:45, and "He who has seen Me has seen the Father," in Jn 14:9) and the Son by the Holy Spirit ("No man can say 'Jesus is the Lord' except by the Holy Spirit," 1 Cor 12:3). Consequently, we only represent what has been revealed to us: the incarnate person of the Son of God, Jesus Christ. The Holy Spirit is represented as It manifested Itself: in the shape of a dove at the baptism of Christ, in the form of tongues of fire at Pentecost, and so on.

If the beginning of the kontakion of the Sunday of Orthodoxy speaks of the divine Incarnation as the basis for the icon, the second part expresses the meaning of the Incarnation and thus the meaning and contents of the New Testament image: "and restored the fallen image to its former state by uniting it to divine beauty."

These words signify that the Son of God, in His Incarnation, recreates and renews in man the divine image soiled by the fall of Adam.[4] Christ, the New Adam, the first-fruits of the new creation, of the celestial man, leads man to the goal for which the original Adam was created. To attain this goal, it was necessary to return to the beginning, to Adam's point of departure. In the Bible we read: "God said: Let us make man in our image, after our likeness" (Gen 1:26). Therefore, according to the plan of the Holy Trinity, man must not only be the image of his Creator, but he must also be a like-image and resemble God. But the description in Genesis of the accomplished creative act no longer mentions the likeness. "So God created man, He made him in the image of God"—κατ' εἰκόνα Θεοῦ (Gen 5:1).[5] One could say that the text insists on the word "image" by repeating it, and the absence of the word "likeness" could not be more evident.[6]

The meaning of the biblical account of the plan of the Holy Spirit to create man "in the image and likeness" of God and the account of the creation "in the image" is understood by the Fathers in the sense that

4 On this subject, see, for example, St Athanasius the Great, *Oratio de incarnatione Verbi*, PG 25:120CD.
5 References are to the Septuagint.
6 On this topic, see V. Lossky, *The Mystical Theology of the Eastern Church*, ch. 6, "Image and Likeness" (New York: St Vladimir's Seminary Press, 1976), 114ff.

man, created in the image of God, is consequently called to realize his likeness to God. To be in the image of God is to have the possibility of acquiring the divine likeness. In other words, this likeness to God is assigned to man as a dynamic task to accomplish.

By baptism, grace restores the image of God to man; as for the divine likeness, grace outlines it later, with the efforts of man to acquire the virtues of which love is the highest, the supreme trait of the likeness to God.

> Just as painters clearly establish the resemblance of the portrait to the model by first tracing the outline in one color, then filling it in little by little with different colors...so also at baptism, the grace of God begins to remake the image to what it was when man came into existence. Then, when we begin to strive with all our will power towards the beauty of the likeness...divine grace makes virtue flourish upon virtue, elevating the beauty of the soul from glory to glory, bestowing upon it the mark of likeness.[7]

Man is a microcosm, a little world. He is the center of created life; and therefore, being in the image of God, he is the means by which God acts in creation. It is precisely in this divine image that the cosmic meaning of man is revealed, according to the commentary of St Gregory of Nyssa. Creation participates in spiritual life through man. Placed by God at the head of all visible creatures, man must realize in himself the union and harmony of everything and unite all the universe to God, in order to make of it a homogeneous organism where God can be "all in all"—for the final goal of creation is its transfiguration.

But man did not accomplish his calling. He turned away from God; his will power weakened, and the inertia in his nature prevailed over his impetus toward God. This led to the disintegration of man, the microcosm, which consequently led to a cosmic disintegration, a catastrophe in all creation. The whole visible world fell into disorder, strife, suffering, death and corruption. This world ceased faithfully to reflect divine beauty, because the divine image, man, inscribed at the center of the universe, was obscured. This was the exact opposite of man's vocation. God's plan, however, did not change. Because man by himself was incapable of reestablishing his nature in its primitive purity, the task which fallen man could no longer fulfill was accomplished by the New

7   Diadochus of Photice, *Oeuvres spirituelles*, ch. 89 (Paris, 1955), 149.

Adam, Christ. St Symeon the New Theologian says the following on this subject:

> Man, such as God had created him, ceased to exist in the world; it was no longer possible for anyone to be like Adam was before his fall. But it was indispensable that such a man exist. God, therefore, wishing there to be a man such as he had created with Adam, sent His only Son to earth, who, having come, became incarnate, assuming perfect humanity in order to be a perfect God and a perfect Man, and in order that the divinity could have a man worthy of Him. This is the Man. There has never been and never will be one like Him. But why was Christ like this? To keep the law and the commandments of God, and to fight and conquer the devil.[8]

To save man from the ascendancy of original sin, it was therefore necessary to have a man such as God had created in the beginning, that is, a sinless man, because sin is an external thing, superimposed on human nature. It is a contrivance of the created will, according to St Gregory of Nyssa, a voluntary denial by creation of the fullness of life.

The Incarnation of the Son of God is not only the re-creation of man in his primitive purity. It is also the realization of that which the first Adam did not know how to achieve. In the words of the Fathers of the Seventh Ecumenical Council: "God re-created man in immortality, thus bestowing upon him a gift which could no longer be taken away from him. This re-creation was more God-like and better than the first creation; it is an eternal gift."[9] This gift of immortality is the possibility of attaining beauty and divine glory—"By uniting it to divine beauty," says the kontakion. By assuming human nature, Christ impregnated it with grace, making it participate in divine life, and cleared the way to the Kingdom of God for man, the way of deification and transfiguration. The divine image was reinstated in man in the perfect life of Christ. He destroyed the power of original sin by His freely-accepted passion and led man to realize the task for which he was created: to achieve divine likeness. In Christ, this likeness is realized to a total, perfect degree by the deification of human nature. Indeed, the deification represents a perfect harmony, a complete union of humanity and divinity, of human will and divine will. The divine likeness, therefore, is only possible for a renewed

---

8   Homily attributed to St Symeon the New Theologian, *Homilies, First Oration*, 3rd Russian edition (Moscow, 1892), 23.
9   Fifth Session, Mansi XIII, 216A.

man, in whom the image of God is purified and restored. This possibility is realized in certain properties of human nature and particularly in its freedom. The attainment of divine likeness is not possible without freedom, because it is realized in a living contact between God and man. Man consciously and freely enters into the plan of the Holy Trinity and creates in himself the likeness to God to the extent of his possibilities and with the help of the Holy Spirit. Thus the Slavonic word *prepodobnyi*, which literally means "very similar," is applied to the monastic type of holiness.[10] The rebirth of man consists in changing "the present humiliated state" of his nature, making it participate in the divine life, because, according to the classical phrase of St Gregory the Theologian, who echoes St Basil the Great, "Man is a creature, but he is commanded to become God." Henceforth, by following Christ, by integrating himself to His body, man can reestablish in himself the divine likeness and make it shine forth in the universe. In the words of St Paul, "We all, with unveiled face, beholding the glory of the Lord, are being changed into His likeness from one degree of glory to another" (2 Cor 3:18). When the human person attains this goal, he participates in divine life and transforms his very nature. Man becomes the son of God, a temple of the Holy Spirit (1 Cor 6:19). By increasing the gifts of grace, he surpasses himself and elevates himself higher than Adam was before his fall, for not only does he return to man's primitive purity, but he is deified, transfigured, "united to divine beauty"; he becomes God by grace.

This ascension of man reverses the process of the fall and begins to deliver the universe from disorder and corruption, since the deification attained by the saint constitutes the beginning of the cosmic transfiguration to come.

10 This word, created at the time of St Cyril and St Methodius to translate the Greek word ὅσιος, indicates the attainment of divine likeness by man. A corresponding expression does not exist in other languages. The opposite term ("dissimilar"), however, can be traced to a very distant epoch. Plato uses this term in a philosophical sense (ἀνομοιότητος πόντον οὐ τόπον) in his *Politics* to express the "noncorrespondence" of the world to its idea. St Athanasius the Great already uses it in a Christian sense: "He who created the world, seeing it succumb to the storm and in danger of being swallowed up in the place of dissimilitude, seized the helm of the soul and came to its aid by correcting all of its transgressions." St Augustine in his confessions says, "*et inveni me longe esse a Te in regione dissimilitudinis*" (PL 32:742), "and I found that I was far distant from you, in a region of total unlikeness," trans Rex Warner (New York, 1983), 149.

The image of God is ineffaceable in man. Baptism only reestablishes and purifies it. The likeness to God, however, can increase or decrease. Being free, man can assert himself in God or against God. He can, if he wants, become "a child of perdition." Then the image of God grows obscure in him, and in his nature he can achieve an abject dissimilarity, a "caricature" of God.

The future transfiguration of the entire human nature, including that of the body, is revealed to us in the transfiguration of the Lord on Mount Tabor: "He was transfigured before them and His face shone like the sun, and His garments became white as light" (Mt 17:2; Mk 9:1-8; Lk 9:27-36). The Lord no longer appeared to His disciples in His "form of a servant," but as God. The whole body of Christ was transfigured, becoming, so to speak, the luminous clothing of His divinity. In His transfiguration "on Mount Tabor, not only divinity appeared to men, but humanity also appeared in divine glory."[11] And the Fathers of the Seventh Ecumenical Council explain: "Speaking of the nature of the transfiguration, it took place not in such a way that the Word left the human image, but rather in the illumination of this human image by His glory."[12] In the words of St Gregory Palamas: "Thus Christ assumes nothing foreign, nor does He take on a new state, but He simply reveals to His disciples what He is."[13] The transfiguration is a manifestation, perceptible by the whole human being, of the divine glory of the second person of the Holy Trinity, who, in His Incarnation, is inseparable from His divine nature, common to both the Father and the Holy Spirit. United hypostatically, the two natures of Christ remain distinct one from the other ("without mixture or confusion," according to the formulation of Chalcedon), but the divine energies penetrate the humanity of Christ and make His human nature becoming resplendent by transfiguring it in a flash of uncreated light. It is "the Kingdom of God which has come with power" (Mk 9:1). According to the Fathers, Christ showed to His disciples the deified state to which all men are called. Just as the body of our Lord was glorified and transfigured, becoming resplendent with divine glory and infinite light, so also the bodies of the saints are glorified and become luminous, being transfigured by the force of divine grace. St Seraphim of Sarov not only explained,

---

11 Metropolitan Philaret, *Complete Works* (in Russian), "Homily 12" (Moscow, 1873), 99.
12 Sixth Session, Mansi XII, 321CD.
13 *Hagioriticus tomus*, PG 150:1232C.

but directly and visibly revealed this likeness between man and God to Motovilov, by transfiguring himself before his very eyes.[14] Another saint, Symeon the New Theologian, describes his own experience of this divine illumination in the following way: "The man whose soul is all on fire also transmits the glory attained internally to his body, just as a fire transfers its heat to iron."[15]

Just as the iron when it is united with the fire becomes hot and yet remains iron, though it is purified, so also human nature when it comes into contact with grace remains what it is, remains whole: Nothing is lost. On the contrary, it is purified just as the iron is purified when in contact with fire. Grace penetrates this nature, is united with it, and from this point on man begins to live the life of the world to come. This is why one can say that a saint is more fully man than the sinner is. He is free from sin, which is essentially foreign to human nature; he realizes the primordial meaning of his existence; he puts on the incorruptible beauty of the Kingdom of God, in the construction of which he participates with his own life. For this reason beauty, as it is understood by the Orthodox Church, is not the characteristic beauty of a creature. It is a part of the life to come, when God will be all in all: "The Lord reigns, He is clothed with majesty," we hear in the prokeimenon at vespers (Ps 92) on Saturday evening: this is an image of the eternal life to come. St Dionysius the Areopagite calls God "beauty" because, on the one hand, God bestows on every creature a unique beauty, and, on the other hand, He adorns him with another beauty, with the true "divine beauty." Every creature is, so to speak, marked with a seal of its Creator. But this seal is not yet the divine likeness, but only the beauty characteristic of the creature.[16] For man, it can be a path or a means of bringing him closer to God. Indeed, according to St Paul, "ever since the creation of the world, His invisible nature, namely His eternal power and deity, has been clearly perceived in the things that have been made" (Rom 1:20). For the Church, however, the value and the beauty of the visible world lie not in the temporary splendor of its present state, but in its potential transfiguration, realized by man. In other words, true beauty is the radiance of the Holy Spirit, the

14 I. Gorainoff, *Sérafin de Sarov* (Bellefontaine, 1973), 208-14.
15 "Catechesis 83," *Eth. VI, Traités théologiques et éthiques*, Introduction, Critical Text and Notes by J. Darrouzès (Paris, 1967), 128-9.
16 St Dionysius the Areopagite, *De divinis nominibus*, ch. 4, PG 3: 701C.

holiness of and the participation in the life of the world to come.

Thus, the second part of the kontakion leads us to the patristic understanding of the icon and allows us to grasp the profound meaning of Canon 82 of the Quinisext Council. "We represent on icons the *holy flesh* of the Lord."[17] The Fathers of the Seventh Ecumenical Council explain this in the following words:

> Although the catholic Church represents Christ in His human form (μορφή) through painting, it does not separate His flesh from the Divinity which is joined to it....When we make the icon of the Lord, we confess His deified flesh, and we recognize in the icon nothing except an image representing a resemblance to the prototype. It is for this reason that it receives its name; it participates only in this, and is therefore venerable and holy.[18]

St Theodore the Studite explains this even more clearly: "The representation of Christ," he says,

> is not in the likeness of a corruptible man, which is disapproved of by the apostles, but as He Himself had said earlier, it is in the likeness of the incorruptible man, but incorruptible precisely because He is not simply a man, but God who became man.[19]

These words of St Theodore explaining the contents of the icon, and the words of the Fathers of the Seventh Ecumenical Council, reflect the christological teaching of St Gregory the Theologian: "Let us not be deprived of our integral salvation by attributing only bones, veins and the human exterior to the Savior. Let us keep man in his entirety and add the divinity."[20]

By comparing these texts, we see that the task of the New Testament image, as the Fathers understood it, consists precisely in portraying as faithfully and completely as possible the truth of the divine Incarnation, insofar as this can be done by art. The image of the man Jesus is the image of God; this is why the Fathers of the Seventh Ecumenical Council, having His icon in mind, say: "In the same Christ, we contemplate both the inexpressible and the represented."[21]

As we see, therefore, the icon is an image not only of a living but also of a deified prototype. It does not represent the corruptible flesh, destined

17 *Epistolae* II, PG 98:157BD.
18 Sixth Session, Mansi XIII, 344.
19 *Adversus iconomachos capita VII*, ch. 1, PG 99: 488.
20 *Ad Cledonium contra Apollinarium epistola I*, PG 37:184AB.
21 Sixth Session, Mansi XIII, 244B.

for decomposition, but transfigured flesh, illuminated by grace, the flesh of the world to come (cf. 1 Cor 15:35-46). It portrays the divine beauty and glory in material ways which are visible to physical eyes. The icon is venerable and holy precisely because it portrays this deified state of its prototype and bears His name. This is why grace, characteristic of the prototype, is present in the icon. In other words, it is the grace of the Holy Spirit which sustains the holiness both of the represented person and of his icon, and it is in this grace that the relationship between the faithful and the saint is brought about through the intermediary of the icon of the saint. The icon participates in the holiness of its prototype and, through the icon, we in turn participate in this holiness in our prayers.

The Fathers of the Seventh Ecumenical Council therefore had to distinguish carefully between an icon and a portrait. The latter represents an ordinary human being, the former a man united to God. The icon is distinguishable from the portrait by its very content, and this content calls for specific forms of expression which are characteristic of the icon alone, and which distinguish it from all other images. The icon indicates holiness in such a way that it need not be inferred by our thought but is visible to our physical eyes. As the image of the sanctification of man, the icon represents the reality which was revealed in the transfiguration on Mount Tabor, to the extent that the disciples were able to understand it. This is why the liturgical texts, particularly for the feast of the Holy Face (August 16), set up a parallel between the content of the icon and the transfiguration:

> Falling to the ground on the holy mountain, the greatest of the apostles prostrated themselves upon seeing the Lord reveal the dawn of divine brightness, and now we prostrate ourselves before the Holy Face, which shines forth brighter than the sun...

Or yet again:

> Having illuminated the human image which had grown dark, O Creator, Thou didst reveal it on Mount Tabor to Peter and to the Sons of Thunder: and now bless and sanctify us, O Lord who lovest mankind, by the brightness of Thy most pure image.[22]

This parallel, which can also be illustrated by other texts, is certainly not the fruit of simple, poetic imagination, but it is rather an indication of the spiritual content of the icon. The icon of the Lord shows us that which

22 Second and third stichera, tone 4.

15. *Transfiguration of Christ.*
Russian icon, 16th century.

was revealed to the apostles on Mount Tabor (Fig. 15). We contemplate not only the face of Jesus Christ, but also His glory, the light of divine Truth made visible to our eyes by the symbolic language of the icon, "the accomplishment made clear to everyone by paintings," as was stated at the Quinisext Council.

This spiritual reality of the icon assumes all its practical teaching value in the last phrase of the kontakion of the Triumph of Orthodoxy: "We confess and proclaim our salvation in word and images." Thus the kontakion ends with man's answer to God, with the acceptance and confession of the divine economy of salvation.

It is easy to understand how to confess salvation in words. The confession by deed can be understood as the accomplishment of the commandments of Christ. But there is something more here. We find the clearest explanation of these words in the Synodicon of the Triumph of Orthodoxy, about which we spoke earlier. This Synodicon[23] contains a series of anathemas against the heretical iconoclasts and a series of proclamations of eternal memory for the confessors of Orthodoxy. Among others, paragraph three proclaims eternal memory "to those who believe and who substantiate their words with writings and *their deeds with representations*, for the propagation and affirmation of the truth by word and images." The representations imply, therefore, that there are deeds which should be represented. But the act of creating images is also a "deed." This word takes on a double meaning in the kontakion: that of internal and external deeds. In other words, it expresses the living experience of the Church, the experience which is expressed in words or in images by the men who attained holiness. On the one hand, man can

23 The oldest text of this Synodicon to have come down to us is a copy made in the sixteenth century of an eleventh-century text. This text, called the Madrid text, was published by Th. Ouspensky in 1891, in Russian (*Otcherki vizantiiskoi obrazovannosti*, 89). The seven paragraphs of this text summarize the entire dogmatic teaching on the icon, concluding with a proclamation of "Memory eternal" to those of the Orthodox faith. In counterpoint, five other paragraphs note the confessional errors and anathematize those who distort true doctrine. In the Russian church during the seventeenth century, this Synodicon was modified to such a degree that its entire dogmatic content about the icon disappeared and its meaning was completely changed. The expression of Orthodox teaching was replaced by a series of general statements, for example, support for the Seventh Ecumenical Council, and so forth. This text contains one single passage on the icon which is of little interest, since it is limited to a rejection of the accusation of idolatry. The passage closely resembles a paraphrase of one of the canons of the Council of Trent (1563).

reestablish in and through the grace of the Holy Spirit his likeness to God. He can transform himself by an internal effort (the spiritual *praxis*) and make of himself a living icon of Christ. This is what the Fathers call "an active life," an internal deed. On the other hand, man can also, for the good of others, translate his inner sanctification into images, either visible or verbal: "We proclaim our salvation in word and images," says the kontakion. Man can therefore also create an external icon, making use of matter which surrounds him and which has been sanctified by the coming of God on earth. Certainly, one can express the inner spiritual state by words alone, but such a state is made apparent, visibly confirmed, *shown* by representation. Word and image "point to one another," according to the *oros* of the council.

Everything we have said about the content of the icon can be compared to a text of the First Epistle of St Paul to the Corinthians. This will help us to understand the significance of the icon, for we all see that this text and the icon express the same teaching and the same experience. "How are the dead raised?," asks St Paul. And he answers, "You foolish men! What you sow does not come to life unless it dies. And what you sow is not the body which is to be..." (1 Cor 15:35-38). He compares our mortal body to the grain thrown to the ground. In the course of this present life, the grain must germinate, that is, it must to some extent enter the life to come. Similarly, we must enter the life of the age to come in order to open ourselves to the general resurrection in that form which it pleases God to give us. "What is sown is perishable, what is raised is imperishable. It is sown in dishonor, it is raised in glory. It is sown in weakness, it is raised in power. It is sown a perishable body, it is raised a spiritual body" (1 Cor 15:42-44). Christ, the new Adam, renewed and recreated our human nature in immortality.

> The first man Adam became a living being; the last Adam became a life-giving spirit. But it is not the spiritual which is first but the physical, and then the spiritual. The first man was from the earth, a man of dust; the second man is from heaven. As was the man of dust, so are those who are of heaven. Just as we have borne the image of the man of dust, we shall also bear the image of the man of heaven. I tell you this, brethren: flesh and blood cannot inherit the Kingdom of God, nor does the perishable inherit the imperishable. (1 Cor 15:45-50)

And a little further, the apostle says, "for this perishable nature must put on the imperishable, and this mortal nature must put on immortality"

(1 Cor 15:53). The light of the transfiguration on Mount Tabor is already
the glory of the world to come. For the power which resurrects the saints
after their death is the Holy Spirit. It is the Holy Spirit who, during the
terrestrial life of the saints, vivifies not only their souls but also their
bodies. This is why we say that the icon transmits not the everyday, banal
face of man, but his glorious and eternal face. For the very meaning of the
icon is precisely to depict the heirs of incorruptibility, the heirs of the
Kingdom of God, of which they are the first-fruits from the time of their
life here on earth. The icon is the image of the man in whom the grace
which consumes passions and which sanctifies everything is truly present.
This is why his flesh is represented completely differently from ordinary
corruptible flesh. The icon is a peaceful transmission, absolutely devoid of
all emotional explanation, of a certain spiritual reality. If grace enlightens
the entire man, so that his entire spiritual and physical being is filled by
prayer and exists in the divine light, the icon visibly captures this man
who has become a living icon, a true likeness of God. *The icon does not
represent the divinity. Rather, it indicates man's participation in the divine
life.*[24]

There is, therefore, an organic link between the veneration of saints
and that of the icons. This is why in a theology that has removed the
veneration of saints (Protestantism), the sacred image no longer exists;
and where the concept of holiness differs from that of Orthodoxy, the
image moves away from Tradition.

The analysis of the kontakion of the Triumph of Orthodoxy gives us a
clearer understanding of the double realism of the New Testament sacred
image, a realism about which we have already spoken. Just as the God-
Man, Jesus Christ, "in whom dwells all the fullness of the Godhead

24 One sometimes hears non-Orthodox, and occasionally even certain Orthodox, say that if the
Christian art of the West, that of the Roman Church, leans towards Nestorianism, the
Orthodox icon has nuances of Monophysitism. What we have already said about the content
of the icon permits us to see the absurdity of this statement. Though one can say that western
art is really Nestorian because it represents only the human aspect of the sacred, that is, the
terrestrial reality alone, the Orthodox icon has nothing to do with monophysitism because it
represents neither the divinity nor man absorbed by it. Rather, it represents man in the fullness
of his terrestrial nature, purified from sin and united with the divine life. To accuse Orthodox
art of Monophysitism is to completely misunderstand its content. For the very same reasons,
one could accuse the Holy Scripture or the Orthodox liturgy of Monophysitism, because like
the icon they express a double reality: that of the creature and that of divine grace.

bodily" (Col 2:9), so also the Church, the body of Christ, is both a divine and human system. It unites two realities in itself: the historical, earthly reality and the grace of the Holy Spirit, the reality of the world and that of God. The purpose of sacred art is precisely to bear witness visibly to these two realities. It is realistic in these two meanings, and thus the icon is distinguishable from all other things, just as the Holy Scripture is distinguishable from all other literary works.

The Church piously preserves historical reality in the representation of Christ, the saints and the events of the Bible. Only a surrender to the most concrete history can turn an icon into a possible, personal encounter with the person represented, in the grace of the Holy Spirit. "It is appropriate," Patriarch Tarasius wrote to the emperor and the empress, "to accept the precious icons of Jesus Christ, since He became the perfect man, provided such icons are painted with historic exactness, in conformity with the Gospel story."[25] The characteristic traits of the saints will therefore be carefully preserved, and only such fidelity to the historical truth allows the iconography of the saints to be so stable (Fig. 16 and Fig. 17). Actually, it is not only a matter of transmitting an image consecrated by tradition, but above all of preserving a direct and living link with the person whom the icon represents. This is why it is essential to abide by an image reproducing, to the greatest degree possible, the traits of the person. Obviously, this is not always possible. Like the biographies of the saints, the physical traits of the saints are often more or less forgotten, and it is difficult to reconstruct them. The likeness therefore risks being imperfect. The unskillfullness of the painter can also lessen it. However, it can never disappear completely. An irreducible minimum always remains which provides a link with the prototype of the icon. As St Theodore the Studite writes,

> Even if we grant that the image does not have the same form as the prototype because of insufficient artistic skill, still our argument would not be invalid. For veneration is given to the image not insofar as it falls short of similarity, but insofar as it resembles its prototype.[26]

In other words, what is essential in this case is not what an icon lacks in resemblance to its prototype, but what it has in common with it. The

25 Mansi XIII, 404D.
26 *Antirrheticus III*, ch. 5, PG 99: 421; *On the Holy Icons*, trans. Catharine P. Roth (New York: St Vladimir's Seminary Press, 1981), 104.

16. *St Peter.*
Fresco from the Roman catacomb of Domitilla (4th century).

17. *St Peter.*
Russian icon, 20th century.
Icon painted by Gregory Kroug.

iconographer can limit himself to a few characteristic traits. In the majority of cases, however, the faithfullness to the original is such that a faithful Orthodox can easily recognize the icons of his most revered saints, not to mention those of Christ and the Virgin. And even if some saint is unknown to him, he can always say to which order of sainthood the saint belongs, i.e., whether he is a martyr, a bishop, a monk, etc.

The Orthodox Church has never accepted the painting of icons according to the imagination of the painter or from a living model, which would signify a conscious and total break from the prototype. The name which the icon bears would no longer correspond to the person represented, and this would be a flagrant lie which the Church could not tolerate. (This general rule has frequently been broken or abused in the past few centuries.) In order to avoid falsehood and a break between the image and its prototype, iconographers use old icons and manuals as models. The ancient iconographers knew the faces of the saints as well as they knew those of their close relatives. They painted them either from memory or by using a sketch or a portrait. Indeed, once a person had acquired a reputation for holiness, an image was made of him to distribute among the faithful immediately after his death, before his official canonization and the discovery of his relics.[27] Thus, all kinds of accounts were preserved on icons, and particularly sketches and the evidence of contemporaries.[28]

However, the historical reality alone, even when it is very precise, does

27 While speaking of the portraitist basis of the icon, N. P. Kondakov notes a characteristic case of the use of the portrait as a documentary basis for the icon. In 1558, when the relics of St Nicetas, Archbishop of Novgorod, were discovered intact, a posthumous portrait of the saint was made and sent to the ecclesiastical authorities with the following letter: "By the grace of the saint, lord, we have sent you on paper an image of St Nicetas, bishop...; following this model, lord, order that an icon of the saint be made." This was followed by details describing the outward appearance of St Nicetas, his vestments, and so forth, to complete the portrait drawn on paper (*The Russian Icon* [in Russian], 3, Part One, 18-9).

28 When the living tradition began to disappear, or more exactly, when people began to deviate from it, towards the end of the sixteenth century, the documentation which the iconographers used was systematized. It was then that the manuals appeared with what are called "podlinniki," with and without illustrations. These establish the standard iconography of the saints and the feast days and indicate the principal colors. When they are not illustrated, they contain brief descriptions which characterize the saints and also mention the colors. As documentation, these "podlinniki" are indispensable to iconographers. But in no way can one attribute to them the same significance as to iconographic canons or the holy Tradition, as certain Western authors do.

not constitute an icon. Since the person depicted is a bearer of divine grace, the icon must portray his holiness to us. Otherwise, the icon would have no meaning. If, in representing the human aspect of the incarnate God, the icon portrays only the historical reality, as does, for example, a photograph, this would mean that the Church sees Christ with the eyes of the non-believing crowd which surrounded Him. But according to the commentary of St Symeon the New Theologian, the words of Christ, "he who has seen Me has seen the Father" (Jn 14:9), were addressed only to those who, while looking at Jesus the man, simultaneously contemplated His divinity.

> Indeed, if we were to conceive this vision as it relates to the body, then those who crucified Him and spat upon Him would also have seen the Father; thus, there would be no difference or preference between believers and unbelievers, since all have equally reached, and, evidently, will reach the desired beatitude....[29]

> The "historical Christ," "Jesus of Nazareth," as He appears to the eyes of alien witnesses; this image of Christ, external to the Church, is always surpassed in the fullness of the revelation given to the true witnesses, to the sons of the Church, enlightened by the Holy Spirit. The cult of the humanity of Christ is foreign to eastern tradition; or, rather, this deified humanity always assumes for the Orthodox Christian that same glorious form under which it appeared to the disciples on Mount Tabor: the humanity of the Son, manifesting forth that deity which is common to the Father and the Spirit.[30]

The contemplation of the Church is different from secular vision precisely by the fact that, in the visible, the Church contemplates the invisible; and in the temporal, the eternal, which is revealed to us in worship. Like worship itself, the icon is a revelation of eternity in time. This is why in sacred art the naturalistic portrait of a person can only be a historical document: in no way can it reflect the liturgical image, the icon.

We have said that the icon expresses the spiritual experience of holiness, and there we also see the same authenticity as in the transmittal of the historical reality; we "are surrounded by so great a cloud of witnesses," in the words of St Paul (Heb 12:1), witnesses who communicate this experience of sanctification to us. "One should call these words a narration of things seen, while the term concept (νόημα) is to be applied to an

---

29 Symeon the New Theologian, *Traités théologiques et éthiques*, Introduction, Critical Text and Notes by J. Darrouzès (Paris, 1967), vol. 2, 86-7.
30 V. Lossky, *The Mystical Theology of the Eastern Church* (New York: 1976), 243.

idea born in the mind."[31] Indeed, only a living, personal experience can bring forth the words, forms, colors or lines which truly correspond to what they express. St Symeon continues:

> Anyone who wants to tell something about, say, a house, a town or a place..., even a play..., must have seen and learned its content thoroughly; only then can he speak with plausibility. For, if he has not seen it beforehand, what could he say of his own devising?...Thus, if no one can speak of or give a description of visible, earthly things without having seen them with his own eyes, how then would anyone have the power to speak...about God, things divine and even the saints and servants of God, and about the vision of God which appears ineffably in them? It is the latter which produces in their heart an ineffable strength. Human words do not allow us to say more about it, unless one is illuminated first by the light of knowledge...[32]

The transfiguration of Christ occurred before only three witnesses, the three apostles "capable of receiving" this revelation; and even they only saw this "dawn of divine light" to the extent that they were able (that is, to the extent of their inner participation in this revelation). We can draw an analogy from the lives of the saints. For example, when St Seraphim of Sarov was transfigured before Motovilov, to whom he wished to show the aim of Christian life, he explained to him that he would be able to see this transfiguration only because he participated in it himself to a certain extent. He would not have been able to see the light of grace if he himself had not been enlightened. This also explains why Tradition asserts that the evangelist Luke painted the icons of the Virgin after Pentecost. Without this "light of knowledge" about which St Symeon the New Theologian speaks, without a direct participation in the sanctification and concrete evidence, no science, no technical perfection, no talent can be of much help. Until the Holy Spirit descended upon them, the apostles themselves (who, however, had constantly seen Christ and believed in Him) had no direct experience of sanctification by the Holy Spirit, and consequently they were not able to convey it by word or image. This is why neither Holy Scripture nor a holy image could appear before Pentecost. In the creation of an icon, nothing can replace the personal, concrete experience of grace. Without such personal experience, one can paint icons only by transmitting the experience of those who had it. This is why the Church, through the voice of its councils and its hierarchs, ordains

31 St Symeon, *op. cit.*, 94-5.
32 *Ibid.*, 96-9.

that icons be painted as they were formerly painted by the holy iconographers. "To represent with colors which conform to Tradition," says St Symeon of Thessalonica, "is true painting; it is analogous to a faithful copy of the Scriptures; and divine grace rests upon it, since what is represented is holy."[33] It is necessary to "represent with colors which conform to Tradition," because in Tradition we participate in the experience of the holy iconographers, in the living experience of the Church.

These words, like those of the Seventh Ecumenical Council, emphasize the participation of the image in the holiness and glory of its prototype. The grace of God rests on the image, says St John of Damascus, because

> the saints were filled with the Holy Spirit during their lives. Even after their death the grace of the Holy Spirit lives on inexhaustibly in their souls, in their bodies which are in their tombs, in their writings and in their holy images, not because of their nature, but as a result of grace and divine action.[34]

The grace of the Holy Spirit lives in the image, which "sanctifies the eyes of the faithful," according to the Synodicon of the Triumph of Orthodoxy (par. 4), and which heals both spiritual and corporal illnesses: "We venerate Thy most pure image, by which Thou hast saved us from the servitude of the enemy," we sing at matins on the Feast of the Holy Face, "by representation, Thou healest our illnesses."[35]

The means used by the icon to convey this spiritual quality corresponds perfectly to the state which is to be communicated, and which has been described in words by the holy ascetic Fathers. It is obvious that grace cannot be expressed by any human means. In real life, if we happen to meet a saint, we do not actually see his holiness. "The world does not see the saints, just as a blind man does not see light."[36] Consequently, we cannot represent this holiness, which we do not see; it cannot be portrayed by word, by image, or by any human means. In the icon, it can only be portrayed with the help of forms, colors, and symbolical lines, by an artistic language established by the Church and characterized by strict historical realism. This is why an icon is more than an image representing a certain religious subject, because this same subject can be represented in

33 *Dialogus contra haereses*, ch. 13, PG 155:113D.
34 *De imaginibus oratio I*, 19, PG 94(I):1249CD.
35 Feast of the Holy Face (August 16), Magnification and Ode 7 of the canon.
36 Philaret, Metropolitan of Moscow, *Sermons* (in Russian), vol. 3, "Sermon 57, for the Annunciation" (Moscow, 1874).

different ways. The specific character of an icon consists more particularly in the *how* of the representation, that is, in the means by which the sanctified state of the represented person is portrayed.

The liturgy tells us that in the icon of the Holy Face we prostrate ourselves before the face of the Savior which "shines more brightly than the sun," that we ask to be "enlightened" by the image of Christ (see the stichera for August 16). We must remember that when Scripture or the liturgy make comparisons with the perceptible world to teach us about the spiritual realm, these are only images and not adequate descriptions. Therefore, speaking of the evangelists' account of the Transfiguration of Christ, St John of Damascus justifies the inevitably insufficient comparison between divine grace and the light of the sun, emphasizing that it is impossible to represent the uncreated by means of the created.[37] In other words, the material light of the sun can only be an *image* of the divine, uncreated light, and nothing more.

On the other hand, however, the icon must correspond to sacred texts which are absolutely explicit, when it is not a matter of poetic imagery or of an allegory, but of translating concrete reality. But how is spiritual illumination to be depicted in the icon, a light "which shines brighter than the sun," surpassing, therefore, all the means of representation? By colors? But they are not sufficient to portray the natural light of the sun. How then could they represent the light which surpasses that of the sun?

In the writings of the Fathers, as well as in the lives of the saints, we often find evidence of a certain light which made the faces of the saints shine internally at the moment of their supreme glorification, just as the face of Moses glowed when he descended from the mountain, so much so that he had to cover it because the people could not stand the glare (Ex 34:30; 2 Cor 3:7-8). The icon conveys this phenomenon of light by a halo, which is a precise sign, in an image, of a well-defined event in the spiritual world. The light which shines from the glorified faces of the saints and which surrounds their heads, as well as the upper part of their bodies, naturally has a spherical shape. As Motovilov says, when speaking of the transfiguration of St Seraphim: "Imagine, in the very center of the

---

37 *Homilia in Transfiguratione*, PG 94(III):545-546; see, B. Krivochéine, "L'enseignement ascétique et théologique de saint Grégoire Palamas," *Seminarium Kondakovianum* VIII (Prague, 1936), 135.

18. Sketches of halos.

sun, in the most brilliant burst of its rays, the face of the man who speaks to you."[38] Since it is obviously impossible to represent this light as such, the only way to convey it in painting is to depict a disk, like a pattern, so to speak, of this luminous sphere. It is not a matter of placing a crown above the head of the saint, as is sometimes done in western images, where this crown somehow remains external, but rather of portraying the radiance of the face. The halo is not an allegory, but the symbolical expression of an authentic and concrete reality (Fig. 18). It is an indispensable part of the icon—indispensable yet insufficient. Indeed, it expresses other things besides Christian holiness. The pagans also frequently represented their gods with halos, as well as their emperors, undoubtedly to emphasize the divine nature of the latter.[39] It is not, therefore, this halo alone which

38 I. Gorainoff, *Sérafin de Sarov* (Bellefontaine, 1973), 209.
39 We cannot say what this light symbolizes for the pagans. On the one hand, the Church recognizes a partial revelation outside of itself, and one may then conclude that the mystery of uncreated light could have been revealed to the pagans to a certain extent. In any case, they knew that divinity was connected with light. On the other hand, the writings of the Fathers reveal to us that the phenomenon of light can have a demonic origin as well, because the devil

distinguishes an icon from other images: It is only an iconographic device, an outward expression of holiness, a witness of the light.[40] For even if the halo should be effaced and no longer be visible, an icon still remains an icon, and is clearly distinguishable from all other images. By its forms and by all its colors, it shows us, in a symbolical manner of course, the inner state of the man whose face "shines brighter than the sun." This state of inner perfection is so inexpressible that the Fathers and ascetic writers characterize it only as an absolute silence. The effect of this illumination on human nature and particularly on the body can, however, be described to a certain extent and indirectly represented. St Symeon the New Theologian referred to the image of the fire united with iron. Other ascetics left us more concrete descriptions.

> When prayer is sanctified by divine grace,...the entire soul is drawn towards God by an unknowable force, which pulls the body with it...In the man born to the new life, it is not only the soul, nor the heart alone, but also the flesh which is filled with spiritual consolation and bliss, with the joy of the living God...[41]

And also:

> Incessant prayer and the teaching of the divine Scripture open the spiritual eyes of the heart which see the King of powers, and there is great joy, and the desire of God burns strongly in the soul: then the flesh is also carried away by the effect of the Spirit and the whole man becomes spiritual...[42]

In other words, when the usual state of dissipation, "the thoughts and sensations of the fallen nature, " are replaced in man by silent prayer, and man is illuminated by the grace of the Holy Spirit, the entire human being flows like molten lava in a single burst toward God. The entire human nature is spiritually exalted; and then, according to St Dionysius the Areopagite, "the disorderly is set in order, the formless takes on form, and the man is radiant with a life full of light."[43] Thus "the peace of God, which passes all understanding" (Phil 4:7) lives in man, this peace which characterizes the presence of the Lord Himself. "In the time of Moses and Elias," says St Macarius the Great,

himself sometimes takes on the features of an angel of light.

40 It is something completely different from the square halo which can be seen on certain images. Formerly, this was a way to indicate that the person was painted when still alive.

41 Bishop Ignatius Brianchaninov, *Ascetic Essay,* vol. 1 (in Russian).

42 "A Most Useful Account of Abba Philemon," 3, (in Russian), *Philokalia* (1888), 397.

43 *The Ecclesiastical Hierarchy,* ch. 2, 3, 8, trans. Thomas L. Campbell (New York: University Press of America, 1983), 32.

when God appeared to them, a multitude of trumpets and powers preceded Him and served the majesty of the Lord; but the coming of the Lord Himself was different, manifested by peace, silence and calm. For it is said: "and after the earthquake a fire; but the Lord was not in the fire; and after the fire a still small voice" [1 Kings 19:12]. This shows that the presence of the Lord is made manifest by peace and harmony.[44]

While remaining a creature, man becomes God according to grace. The body of man, as well as his soul, participates in the divine life. This participation does not change him physically: "What we see does not change," says St Gregory of Nyssa. "An old man does not become an adolescent, wrinkles do not disappear. What is renewed is the inner being, soiled by sin and grown old in bad habits. This being returns to its childlike innocence."[45] In other words, the body retains its structure, its biological properties and the characteristic traits of the outward appearance of man. Nothing is lost. Rather, everything is changed, and the body, entirely united with grace, is illuminated by its union with God. "The [Holy] Spirit, uniting with the intellect," says St Anthony the Great,

> ...teaches it to keep the entire body, from head to toe, in order—the eyes, so that they can see purely, the ears so that they can hear in peace..., the tongue, so that it can speak only good, the hands, so that they are put into movement only to be lifted in prayer or to perform works of charity..., the stomach, so that it may keep eating and drinking within appropriate limits..., the feet, so that they may walk aright in the will of God....Thus, the entire body becomes accustomed to goodness and is transformed, by submitting itself to the power of the Holy Spirit, so that it finishes by participating to a certain extent in the characteristics of the spiritual body that it will receive at the resurrection of the just.[46]

The patristic passages just quoted are like so many verbal icons, even to the details which the teaching of St Anthony makes us understand. This is why they are of utmost importance to our subject. The effect of the divine grace on the human body, and in particular on the senses, as described in words by St Anthony, is shown to us in the icon. The analogy between the verbal description and the image is so obvious that it leads us to a very clear conclusion: There is an ontological unity between the ascetic experience of Orthodoxy and the Orthodox icon. It is precisely this experience and its outcome which is described by the Orthodox

44　Russian *Philokalia*, vol. 1 (Moscow, 1877), 192.
45　As quoted by G. Florovsky, *The Fathers of the Fourth and Fifth Centuries* (in Russian) (Westmead, 1972), 171.
46　Russian *Philokalia*, vol. 1, 21.

ascetics who are shown to us in the icons and conveyed by them. With the help of colors, forms and lines, with the help of symbolical realism, an artistic language unique in its genre, the spiritual world of the man who has become a temple of God is revealed to us. The order and inner peace to which the Holy Fathers testify are conveyed in the icon by outward peace and harmony: The entire body of the saint, in every detail, even the hair and the wrinkles, even the garments and all that surrounds him, is unified and restored to a supreme harmony. It is a visible expression of the victory over the inner division and chaos in man and, as we shall see, a victory by man over the division and chaos in humanity and in the world.

The unusual details of appearance which we see in the icon—in particular in the sense organs: the eyes without brilliance, the ears which are sometimes strangely shaped—are represented in a non-naturalistic manner, not because the iconographer is unable to do otherwise, but because their natural state is not what he wants to represent. The icon's role is not to bring us closer to what we see in nature, but to show us a body which perceives what usually escapes man's perception, i.e., the perception of the spiritual world. The questions which St Seraphim of Sarov insistently asked Motovilov as he was transfigured before him illustrate this well: "What do you see?," "What do you feel?," etc. For the light which Motovilov saw, the scent which he smelled, the heat which he felt, were not of the physical order. At that moment, his senses were perceiving the effect that grace has on the physical world which surrounded him. This non-naturalistic manner of representing in the icon the organs of sense conveys the deafness, the absence of reaction to the business of the world, impassiveness, detachment from all excitement and, conversely, the acceptance of the spiritual world by those who have reached holiness. The Orthodox icon is the expression in an image of the following hymn of Holy Saturday: "Let all mortal flesh keep silent...pondering nothing earthly-minded." Everything here is subordinate to the general harmony which expresses peace, order and inner harmony. For there is no disorder in the Kingdom of the Holy Spirit. God is "the God of peace and order," St Symeon the New Theologian says.[47]

Thus, the icon shows us the saint's glorified state, his transfigured,

47 Catechetical Instruction attributed to St Symeon the New Theologian (in Russian), *Prayer*, 15 (Moscow, 1892), 143.

19. *The head of St George the Martyr* (detail).
Novgorod School, about 1400.
Coll. Dr. Amberg, Kölliken, Switzerland.

eternal face (Fig. 19). But it is made for us; given everything that has been said, it should therefore be clear to us that in its coded language the icon speaks to us, in the same way as the patristic passages that were quoted are not concerned only with the ascetic practices of the monks, but of all believers; for the acquisition of grace is a task assigned to all members of the Church. As a manifestation of the ascetic experience of Orthodoxy, the icon has a crucial educational function, and therein lies the essential goal of sacred art. Its constructive role lies not only in the teaching of the truths of the Christian life, but in the education of the whole person.

The content of the icon forms a true spiritual guide for the Christian life and, in particular, for prayer. Prayer is a conversation with God; this is why it requires the absence of passions, deafness to and the non-acceptance of external, worldly excitement. "And thus, brothers," St Gregory the Theologian says,

> let us not perform what is holy in an impure manner, what is sublime in a lowly fashion, what is worthy of honor in a disgraceful way, and, in short, what is holy in a terrestrial manner....With us all things are somehow holy: activity, movement, desire, speaking, as well as our manner of walking and our garments, even our gestures, because reason (λόγος) extends to everything and guides man according to God; this is how our celebration is spiritual and solemn.[48]

This is precisely what is shown by the icon. A reasonable guide for our senses is indispensable, for through them evil enters the human soul: "The purity of man's heart is disturbed by the disordered movement of images which enter and leave by the senses of sight, hearing, touch, taste and smell, as well as the spoken word," says St Anthony the Great.[49] This is why the Fathers speak of the five senses as the "doors" of the soul: "Close all the doors of your soul, that is, your senses," St Isaiah teaches, "and guard them carefully, so that your soul does not accidentally go wandering through them, or so that neither the cares nor the words of the world drown out the soul." Praying before an icon or simply looking at it, we are constantly reminded of what St Isaiah speaks: "He who believes that his body will be resurrected on the judgment day must keep it without sin and free from all stain and vice."[50] We must do this so that, in our prayer at least, we close the doors of our soul and strive to teach our body (as the

---

48 St Gregory the Theologian, *Oratio XI*, PG 35:840A.
49 Russian *Philokalia*, vol., 1, 122.
50 Abba Isaiah, *Homily 15*, Russian *Philokalia*, vol. 1, 33.

saint in the icon taught his body) to keep itself aright in and by the grace
of the Holy Spirit, so that our eyes may "see with purity," so that "our ears
may hear in peace," and so that our "heart does not nurture evil
thoughts." In other words, by the image, the Church endeavors to help us
redeem our nature which has been tainted by sin.

In the ascetic domain, that of prayer, the Fathers describe the Orthodox spiritual experience by using the image of "the narrow gate...that
leads to life" (Mt 7:14). It is as if man were standing at the opening of a
road which, instead of leading into space, opens up into infinite fullness.
A door that opens into the divine life is opened for the Christian. This is
how St Macarius, like many other ascetic authors, speaks of spiritual
progress: "Doors are opened...and man enters the interior of many
abodes; and as he enters, still other doors are opened before him, and he
is enriched; and to the degree that he is enriched, new marvels are shown
to him..."[51] Once embarked on the path to which leads the narrow gate,
man sees endless possibilities and perspectives opening before him, and
his path, far from becoming narrow, becomes wider. But in the beginning, it is but a simple point in our hearts, from which our whole
perspective must be reversed. This is the authentic and literal meaning of
the Greek word μετάνοια, which means "change of mind."

Thus, the icon is both a means and a path to follow. It is itself a prayer.
Visibly and directly, it reveals to us this freedom from passion about
which the Fathers speak. It teaches us "to fast with our eyes," in the words
of St Dorotheus.[52] And indeed, it is impossible "to fast with our eyes"
before just any image, be it abstract, or even an ordinary painting. Only
the icon can portray what it means "to fast with our eyes" and what this
allows us to attain.

Thus, the aim of the icon is not to provoke or glorify in us a natural
human feeling. It is not "moving," not sentimental. Its intention is to
attune us to the transfiguration of all our feelings, our intelligence and all
the other aspects of our nature, by stripping these of all exaltation which
could be harmful or unhealthy. Like the deification which it conveys, the
icon suppresses nothing that is human: neither the psychological element,
nor a person's various characteristics in the world. Thus the icon of a saint

51 Russian *Philokalia,* vol. 1, 230.
52 *Teachings and Messages Useful to the Soul* (in Russian), 7th ed. (Optina Pustyn, 1895), 186.

20. *The Virgin with Child.*
16th century Russian icon.

21. *Madonna del Granduca*
by Raphael

does not fail to indicate his occupation in the world, which he was able to turn into a spiritual activity, whether an ecclesiastic occupation such as that of a bishop or a monk, or a worldly activity, such as that of a prince, a soldier or a physician. But, as in the Gospel, this burden of activities—thoughts, learning, and human feelings—is represented in its contact with the divine world; this contact purifies everything and consumes that which cannot be purified. Every manifestation of human nature, each phenomenon of life, is illumined, becomes clear, acquires its true meaning and place.

Just as we represent the God-Man as being similar to us in all things *except sin*, so do we represent the saint like a person freed from sin. According to St Maximus the Confessor,

> Our flesh, like the flesh of Christ, is also freed from the corruption of sin. For just as Christ was without sin through His Flesh and His soul as a Man, so can we who believe in Him and who have put on Christ through the Spirit, be in Him without sin, through our will.[53]

The icon shows us precisely the body of a holy person, "in the mould of His glorious body" (Phil 3:21), a body freed from the corruption of sin, which "in a certain manner partakes of the properties of the spiritual body it will receive at the resurrection of the just."

Orthodox sacred art is a visible expression of the dogma of the Transfiguration. The transfiguration of man is understood and transmitted here as a well-defined, objective reality, in full accordance with Orthodox teaching. What is shown to us is not an individual interpretation or an abstract or more-or-less deteriorated understanding, but a truth taught by the Church (Fig. 20 and Fig. 21).

The colors of the icon convey the color of the human body, but not the natural flesh tints, which, as we have seen, simply do not correspond to the meaning of the Orthodox icon. Also, much more is involved than depicting the physical beauty of the human body. The beauty in the icon is spiritual purity, inner beauty and, in the words of St Peter, "let it be the hidden person of the heart, with the imperishable jewel of a gentle and quiet spirit, which in God's sight is very precious" (1 Pet 3:4). It is the beauty of the communion of the terrestrial with the celestial. It is this beauty-holiness, this divine likeness attained by man, that the icon por-

53 *Active and Contemplative Chapters* (in Russian), ch. 67, *Philokalia*, vol. 3, 263.

trays. In its own language, the icon conveys the work of grace which, according to St Gregory Palamas, "paints in us, so to speak, on what is the image of God that which is in the divine likeness, in such a way that...we are transformed into His likeness."[54]

The justification and the value of the icon do not, therefore, lie in its beauty as an object, but in that which it represents—an image of beauty in the divine likeness.

It is understandable that the light of the icon which enlightens us is not the natural brightness of faces depicted by color, but rather the divine grace which purifies man, the light of purified and sinless flesh. This light of the sanctified flesh must not be understood only as a spiritual phenomenon, nor as a uniquely physical phenomenon, but as the two together, a revelation of the spiritual flesh to come (Fig. 22).[55]

The clothing, while keeping its distinctiveness and covering the body in a perfectly logical fashion, is represented in such a way so as not to conceal the glorified state of the saint. It emphasizes the work of man and becomes in some way the image of his vestment of glory, of his "robe of incorruptibility." The ascetic experience, or rather its result, also finds here its outward expression in the severity of the often geometrical forms, in the lighting and in the lines of the folds. They cease to be disordered. They change their appearance and acquire a rhythm and an order which is subordinate to the general harmony of the image. In effect, the sanctification of the human body is communicated to its clothing. We know that touching the clothing of Christ, the Virgin, of the apostles and the saints brought healing to the faithful. One

54 *Philokalia*, vol. 5 (Moscow, 1889), 300-1, "To the Nun Xenia, on the Virtues and the Passions" (in Russian).

55 This is why the problem of representing the human body never arose in Orthodoxy as in Roman Catholicism after the decision of the Council of Trent (25th Session): "The Holy Council wishes that all impurity be avoided, that images not be given provocative charms." The "impurity" that had to be avoided was the human body. This is why the first thing that the Roman ecclesiastical authorities did was to prohibit the representation of the naked body in religious art. A real purge against nudity began. By order of Pope Paul IV, the figures of Michelangelo's Last Judgment were veiled. Pope Clement VIII, renouncing half-measures, decided to have the whole fresco obliterated, and was only stopped by the entreaties of the Academy of St Luke. Charles Borromeo, who firmly believed in the decisions of the Council of Trent, had the nude obliterated whenever he found it. Paintings and statues which did not seem modest enough were destroyed (see E. Mâle, *L'art religieux après le Concile de Trente* [Paris, 1932], 2). Painters themselves burned their own works. The very character of sacred art in the Orthodox Church would make such a situation impossible.

22. *St Basil the Blessed.*
20th century Russian icon.
Icon painted by Leonid Ouspensky

need only recall the Gospel story of the hemorrhaging woman or the healings that took place through the clothing of St Paul (Acts 19:12).

The inner order of the man represented in the icon is naturally reflected in his posture and in his movements. The saints do not gesticulate. They are in prayer before the face of God, and each of their movements and the very posture of their bodies take on a hieratic, sacramental aspect. Usually, they are fully turned towards the spectator, or at least partially turned. This trait characterizes Christian art from its origins, as we have seen when we studied the art of the catacombs. The saint is present before us and not somewhere in space. Addressing our prayer to him, we must see him face to face. This is without a doubt the reason why the saints are almost never represented in profile, except in very rare cases when they are turned towards the center in complicated works. A profile does not allow direct contact; it is, as it were, the beginning of absence. This is why only persons who have not yet attained holiness are represented in profile, such as the wise men and the shepherds in the icon of the Nativity, for example.

It is the nature of holiness to sanctify that which surrounds it. It is in man and through man that the participation of all creatures in the divine eternal life is actualized and made manifest. Just as creation fell with the fall of man, so is it saved by the deification of man, for

> it was not for its own purposes that creation had frustration imposed upon it, but for the purposes of him who imposed it, with the intention that the whole creation itself might be freed from its slavery to corruption and brought into the same glorious freedom as the children of God. (Rom 8:20-23)

We have a sign which marks the beginning of the restoration of unity in the entire fallen creation. This is the sojourn of Christ in the desert: "He was with the wild beasts, and the angels served him" (Mk 1:13). The heavenly and earthly creatures destined to become the new creation in the God-Man Jesus Christ are assembled around Him. The thought of the unification in peace of the entire universe clearly informs all Orthodox iconography.[56] This union of all creatures, beginning with the angels down to the inferior creatures, is the renewed universe to come; in the icon, it is contrasted to the general discord, to the prince of this world.

---

56 It is most particularly emphasized in certain icons which reveal the cosmic meaning of creation—for example, "Let everything that breathes praise the Lord," or "All creation rejoices in you," and others.

23. *St Blaise and St Spyridon, protectors of animals.*
14th century Russian icon.

Peace and harmony restored, the Church embracing the entire world—this is the central idea of Orthodox sacred art, which dominates architecture as well as painting.[57] This is why, in the icon, we find that everything which surrounds a saint changes its mien. The world that surrounds man—the bearer and announcer of the divine revelation—here becomes an image of the world to come, transformed and renewed. Everything loses its usual disorderly aspect, everything becomes a harmonious structure: the landscape, the animals, architecture. Everything that surrounds the saint bows with him to a rhythmic order. Everything reflects the divine presence, is drawn—and also draws us—towards God. The earth, the world of vegetation and the animal world are represented in the icon, not to bring us close to what we always see around us—a fallen world in its corruptible state—but to show that this world participates in the deification of man. The effect of holiness on the entire created world, especially on the wild animals, is often seen in the saints' lives (Fig. 23).[58] Epiphanius, a disciple and biographer of St Sergius of Radonezh, comments as follows on the attitude of wild beasts toward the saint: "Let no one be astonished, for you know that when God dwells in a man and when the Holy Spirit rests in him, everything submits to him as to Adam before his fall, when Adam lived alone in the desert." The life of St Isaac the Syrian states that the animals who came to him smelled in him the odor which Adam exhaled before his fall. This is why, when animals are represented in an icon, they have an unusual appearance. While preserving the characteristic traits of their species, they lose their usual appearance. This would seem to be odd or awkward if we did not understand the profound language of the iconographers, who allude here to the mystery of paradise which is, at the moment, inaccessible to us.

As for architecture in the icon, while subordinate to the general harmony, it plays a particular role. Like the landscape, it identifies the place where the event takes place: a church, a house, a town. But the building (just like the cave of the Nativity or that of the Resurrection) never encloses the scene. It only acts as a background, so that the event does not occur *in* the building, but *in front of* it. This is because the very meaning of the events that the icons represent is not limited to their

57 E. Trubetskoi, *The Meaning of Life* (in Russian) (Berlin, 1922), 71-2.
58 For example, those of St Isaac the Syrian, St Mary of Egypt, St Sergius of Radonezh, St Seraphim of Sarov, St Paul of Obnorsk and many others.

24. *The Annunciation.*
16th century Russian icon.
Icon Museum, Recklinghausen.

historical place, just as, while having taken place in time, they surpass the moment when they occurred. It is only since the beginning of the seventeenth century that Russian iconographers, under the influence of western art, have begun representing scenes which take place within a building. The architecture is linked with the human figures in the general meaning of the image and in its composition, but the logical connection is often completely missing. If we compare the way in which architecture is represented, we will see a great difference. The human body, although represented in a manner which is not naturalistic, is, however, with very rare exceptions completely logical: Everything is in its place. The same is true of clothing: The way in which garments are treated, in which the folds fall, is quite logical. But the architecture frequently defies all human logic, both in its forms and in its details (Fig. 24). If real architectural forms are the starting point, proportion is absolutely neglected, the doors and windows are not in their proper place and, besides, are completely useless because of their dimensions, etc. Contemporary opinion sees many Byzantine and antique forms in the icon, due to a blind attachment of the iconographers to forms which have become incomprehensible. But the true meaning of this phenomenon is that the action represented in the icon transcends the rationalistic logic of men and the laws of earthly life. Architecture, be it antique, Byzantine or Russian, is the element which best permits the icon to portray this. It is arranged with a certain pictorial "foolishness for the sake of Christ," in complete contradiction to "the spirit of gravity." Such architectural fantasy systematically frustrates reason, puts it back in its place, and emphasizes the meta-logical character of faith.[59]

The strange and unusual character of the icon is the same as that of the Gospel. For the Gospel is a true challenge to every order, to all the wisdom of the world. "I will destroy the wisdom of the wise, and the cleverness of the clever I will thwart," says the Lord by the mouth of His prophets whom St Paul quotes (1 Cor 1:21). The Gospel calls us to life in Christ; the icon represents this life. This is why it sometimes uses irregular and shocking forms, just as holiness sometimes tolerates extreme forms which

59 The alogical character of architecture continued until the period of decadence (end of the sixteenth-beginning of the seventeenth centuries), when the understanding of iconographic language was gradually lost. From that time on, architecture became logical and proportioned. What is amazing is that today one finds truly fantastic masses of architectural forms.

seem like madness in the eyes of the world, such as the holiness of the fools in Christ. "They say that I am mad," said one of them, "but without madness one does not enter into the Kingdom of God...To live according to the Gospel one must be mad. As long as men are reasonable and of sober mind, the Kingdom of God will not come to earth."[60] Madness for the sake of Christ and the sometimes provocative forms of icons express the same evangelical reality. Such an evangelical perspective inverts that of the world. The universe shown to us by the icon is one which is ruled not by rational categories or by human standards, but by divine grace. Hence the hieratic nature of the icon, its simplicity and majesty, its quietness; hence also the rhythm of its lines and the joy of its colors. It reflects the ascetic effort and the joy of victory. It is sorrow transformed into the "joy of the living God." It is the new order in the new creation.

The world which we see here no longer reflects its daily banality. The divine light penetrates everything, and this is why the persons and the objects are not illuminated from one side or another by a source of light; they do not project shadows, because there are no shadows in the Kingdom of God, where everything bathes in light. In the technical language of iconographers, "light" is called the background of the icon. We will speak of this later on.

In this study, we have tried to show that, just as the symbolism of the first centuries of Christianity was a language common to the entire Church, so also the icon is a language common to the entire Church because it expresses the common Orthodox teaching, the common Orthodox ascetic experience and the common Orthodox liturgy. The sacred image has always expressed the revelation of the Church, bearing it in a visible form to the faithful, placing it before their eyes as an answer to their questions, a teaching and a guide, as a task to accomplish, as a prefiguration and the first-fruits of the Kingdom of God. Divine revelation and its acceptance by man are the same action in two ways, so to speak. Apocalypse and gnosis, the path of revelation and that of knowledge, correspond to each other. God descends and reveals Himself to man; man responds to God by lifting himself, by harmonizing his life with the attained revelation. In the image he receives the revelation, and by the image he responds to this revelation to the degree that he partici-

60 Archimandrite Spiridon, *Mes Missions en Sibérie* (Paris: Editions du Cerf, 1950), 39-40.

pates in it. In other words, the icon is a visible testimony to the descent of God to man as well as to the impetus of man towards God. If the word and the song of the Church sanctify our soul by means of hearing, the image sanctifies by means of sight, which is, according to the Fathers, the most important of the senses. "The eye is the lamp of the body. So, if your eye is sound, your whole body will be full of light" (Mt 6:22). By word and by image, the liturgy sanctifies our senses. Being an expression of the image and likeness of God restored in man, the icon is a dynamic and constructive element of worship.[61] This is why the Church, by the decision of the Seventh Ecumenical Council, orders that icons be placed "on the same level as the images of the life-giving cross, in all of the churches of God, on vases and sacred vestments, on the walls, on wooden boards, in homes and in the streets." In the icon, the Church recognizes one of the means which can and must allow us to realize our calling, that is, to attain the likeness of our divine prototype, to accomplish in our life that which was revealed and transmitted to us by the God-Man. The saints are very few in number, but holiness is a task assigned to all men, and icons are placed everywhere to serve as examples of holiness, as a revelation of the holiness of the world to come, a plan and a project of the cosmic transfiguration. Furthermore, since the grace attained by the saints during their lives continues to dwell in their image,[62] these images are placed everywhere for the sanctification of the world by the grace which belongs to them. Icons are like the markers on our path to the new creation, so that, according to St Paul, in contemplating "the glory of the Lord, [we] are being changed into His likeness" (2 Cor 3:18).

Men who have known sanctification by experience have created images which correspond to it and which truly constitute a "revelation and demonstration of that which is hidden," in the words of St John of Damascus, just as the tabernacle does, following the directions of Moses, revealing what had been shown to him on the mountain. These images not only reveal a transfigured universe to man, but they also allow him to participate in it. It can be said that the icon is painted according to nature, but with the help of symbols, because the nature which it represents is not directly representable. It is the world which will only be fully revealed at

61 It is far from being merely conservative and having a passive function only, as certain outside observers think.
62 St John of Damascus, *De imaginibus oratio I*, ch. 19, PG 94(1):1249CD.

the second coming of the Lord.

So far, we have explained the content of the icon as an expression of dogma and as the fruit of the Orthodox spiritual experience during the christological period in the history of the Church, a content highlighted by the Fathers and by the councils, and especially by the dogma of the veneration of icons. We will now explain succinctly how the content of the icon developed and became more precise through its classical artistic language; we shall also consider the role played by the icon during the centuries that followed, including in our time.